BRUSH WITH A BODY

A Play in Three Acts

by Maurice McLoughlin

SAMUEL FRENCH

samuelfrench.co.uk

ISBN 978-0-573-01058-3

www.samuelfrench.co.uk
www.samuelfrench.com

For Amateur Production Enquiries

United Kingdom and World excluding North America

plays@samuelfrench.co.uk

020 7255 4302/01

Each title is subject to availability from Samuel French, depending upon country of performance.

BRUSH WITH A BODY

Produced by City Stage Productions Ltd and Anna Deere Wiman at the St Martin's Theatre, London, on the 19th July 1962, with the following cast of characters:

(in the order of their appearance)

SARAH WALLING	*Bernadette Milnes*
CYNTHIA WALLING, her sister	*Joyce Marlow*
MR FLAHERTY, an Irish chimney-sweep	*Patrick McAlinney*
MRS D'ARCY, the Wallings' housekeeper	*Gladys Henson*
HENRY WALLING, the brother	*Jack Watling*
PAUL MARTELL, a young actor	*Raymond Smith*
SYBIL WALLING, the mother	*Mary Merrall*
DETECTIVE INSPECTOR HARDY	*J. Grant Anderson*
SERGEANT BRAY	*Gordon Cave*
ROSITA HERNANDEZ	*Gilgi Hauser*
THE HON. PAMELA COLEFAX, Henry's fiancée	*Pat Gilber*

Directed by RICHARD DALE

Setting by JOHN BARRIE

SYNOPSIS OF SCENES

The action of the Play passes in the morning-room of Sybil Walling's house in Hampstead

ACT I
A summer morning

ACT II
The next morning

ACT III
Immediately following

Time—the present

To face page 1—Brush With a Body

ACT I

SCENE—*The morning-room of Sybil Walling's house in Hampstead. A summer morning.*

It is a large, rambling, three-storied house. Double doors R *lead to the entrance hall and stairs. A door up* L *leads to the kitchen and back entrance to the house. Up* C *there is a large window with a glass-panelled door leading to a high-walled garden, which has access to the back and side entrances to the house. The fireplace is* L. *Up* RC *there is a round dining-table with two upright chairs* R *and* L *of it. A small table with a telephone on it stands above the doors* R *and an upright chair is down* R. *Easy chairs stand* RC *and down* L, *with a sofa to match* LC. *There is a sideboard up* C, *a low coffee-table down* C, *and a table behind the sofa.*

When the CURTAIN *rises,* SARAH WALLING *is seated* L *of the dining-table finishing her breakfast. She is aged about nineteen. She is reading a copy of "The Stage" and has a transistor radio on the table beside her, playing a "pop" number. Her table-napkin is on the floor beside her.* CYNTHIA WALLING, *her elder sister, enters from the hall.* CYNTHIA *is in her late twenties. She carries a drawer containing a quantity of old papers, etc.*

CYNTHIA. Haven't you finished yet, Sarah?

SARAH (*without looking up*) Nearly.

CYNTHIA (*crossing to the table behind the sofa*) Hurry, then, and turn that thing off. (*She puts the drawer on the table*)

SARAH. Cynthia dear, just try to remember while you're on holiday that I'm not a member of your sixth form.

CYNTHIA (*looking at the papers in the drawer*) I hope my sixth form have more sense than to sit about at this time in the morning listening to that noise. Turn it *off*.

SARAH. That record was requested by two Horsham housewives *and* a schoolteacher in Sutton Coldfield—I can't think why. (*She switches off the transistor*)

CYNTHIA. Has Mrs D'Arcy arrived?

SARAH. Haven't seen her.

CYNTHIA. She knows we have the sweep coming—I asked her to be early. I'll look through this later. I can't believe mother really wants all this old stuff of father's. (*She moves to* L *of Sarah*)

SARAH. Ask her when she comes home.

CYNTHIA. She'll say "yes", and then we'll never get rid of it.

SARAH. I think it's unfair changing her room while she's away. She might not like it.

(CYNTHIA *picks up Sarah's napkin, rolls it, puts it in its ring and lays it on the table*)

CYNTHIA. It will be much better for her. Henry says so.

SARAH (*pouring coffee*) Henry doesn't care, he hardly ever sees her. When he doesn't stay at his consulting rooms, he's off watching that ghastly Pamela Colefax prancing all over England on a horse. (*She finishes her toast*)

CYNTHIA. Sarah!

SARAH. He might as well be engaged to a centaur.

CYNTHIA. Don't be ridiculous. Finish your coffee then clear the table. If Mrs D'Arcy comes send her up to me. (*She crosses to the hall door*) You can come, too.

SARAH. I'm supposed to be meeting Paul Martell this morning.

CYNTHIA. He'll have to wait until we've finished.

SARAH. Oh!

(CYNTHIA *exits to the hall.* SARAH *rises, picks up her cup of coffee and takes it with her paper to the sofa. She puts the coffee on the floor beside the sofa, sits on the sofa, puts her feet up and reads her paper.*

MR FLAHERTY *appears outside the open garden door and taps on it. He is in his fifties, is scruffily dressed in overalls and has a slightly sooty face. He has a copy of the "New Statesman" sticking out of his pocket*)

FLAHERTY. Dermot Ignatius Eamon McMorragh Flaherty, for to sweep your chimneys. Will I come in?

SARAH. Hello.

FLAHERTY. Me cart's be the side gate there. Will I bring me brushes in?

SARAH. You'd better see my sister, she's the organizer around here.

FLAHERTY (*coming into the room*) Is the chimney upstairs or down?

SARAH. Up. I'll go and tell her when I've finished my coffee. Do you want a cup?

FLAHERTY (*moving to the table*) Coffee is it? Do you have any tea?

SARAH. Not with breakfast.

FLAHERTY. Ah, well. Don't bother, I'll pour it meself. (*He pours a cup of coffee*)

(SARAH *returns to her paper*)

Ye haven't finished your toast.

SARAH. No. Would you like it?

FLAHERTY. It's a bit burnt, but never mind. (*He butters a piece of toast*) Do you have any lemon marmalade?

SARAH (*looking up at him*) No.

FLAHERTY (*spreading marmalade on his toast*) A pity, I don't care for orange. All them bright bits of peel in it, y'know. (*He puts the toast on a plate, picks up his cup of coffee and takes toast and coffee to the easy chair* RC) I like the lemon stuff with a golliwog on the lid. (*He settles himself in the easy chair*)

(SARAH *watches, fascinated*)

Nice place you've got here. (*He takes out his "New Statesman" and puts on his spectacles. He takes a swig of coffee and a bite of toast as he reads*)

(SARAH, *by this time, is almost on the edge of her seat*)

SARAH. Are you quite comfortable?

FLAHERTY. Oh, yes. What d'ye think Sir Alfred Munnings would have said about Picasso's Blue Period?

SARAH. I beg your pardon?

FLAHERTY. 'Tis a competition in the *New Statesman.*

SARAH. Oh.

FLAHERTY. Listen to this. (*He reads*) "Let us imagine", it says, "that Sir Alfred Munnings had been asked to write the foreword to the catalogue of a Picasso exhibition and *vice versa.* Readers are invited to submit their ideas of the results. Entries should not exceed five hundred words." That'd be two hundred and fifty words each, I suppose.

SARAH. I wouldn't know.

FLAHERTY. You don't go in for these competitions?

SARAH. Not even if they're five words each.

(CYNTHIA *enters briskly from the hall*)

CYNTHIA (*as she enters*) Sarah, I've been thinking . . . (*She stops as she sees Flaherty*)

FLAHERTY (*rising*) Good day to ye, ma'am.

CYNTHIA. Are you the sweep?

FLAHERTY. I am. Dermot Ignatius Eamon McMorragh Flaherty. (*He resumes his seat*)

SARAH. We were doing a competition in the *New Statesman.*

CYNTHIA (*crossing to* R *of the sofa*) You were what?

FLAHERTY. Sure I won meself a book token not a month since.

CYNTHIA. Could you postpone this week's entry until you've swept the chimney?

FLAHERTY. We'll discuss it later. (*He feels around his mouth with his tongue*) One o' them bits of peel is stuck in me tooth. (*He rises and takes his cup back to the table*) The coffee was on the cold side, too.

CYNTHIA. I'm sorry your breakfast wasn't satisfactory, Mr Flaherty.

FLAHERTY. Ah sure, how were you to know I was coming for a cup of coffee. (*He moves up* C) Will I bring me cart round to the front door?

CYNTHIA. No. (*She picks up Flaherty's plate and puts it on the table*) Bring your things through here.

(FLAHERTY *turns to go*)

I don't want a mess at the front.

FLAHERTY (*stopping and turning*) Did I hear the word "mess" from your lips? I could dance all over your house with a bag of soot under each arm and a brush balanced on the tip o' me nose and not a fleck of soot would ye find.

(FLAHERTY *exits by the garden door*)

CYNTHIA (*moving to* R *of the sofa*) What are you thinking about, Sarah? You know what there is to be done and here you are reading the *New Statesman* with the sweep.

SARAH. What was Picasso's Blue Period?

CYNTHIA. Would you please clear that breakfast table.

(*The front door off* R *is heard to open and close*)

MRS D'ARCY (*off*) It's only me.

CYNTHIA. Thank goodness. That's Mrs D'Arcy.

(SARAH *rises, crosses to the table and reluctantly stacks the crockery on the tray.*

MRS D'ARCY *enters from the hall. She is in her fifties and is dressed very smartly in a picture hat and costume. She has a very prominent nose*)

MRS D'ARCY (*crossing to* R *of Cynthia*) I'm sorry I'm late.

CYNTHIA. Mrs D'Arcy, you're very late. I particularly wanted you here early. (*She collects Sarah's coffee-cup from the floor*)

MRS D'ARCY. I'm sorry, Miss Walling. I was just coming out to come when this arrived. (*She flourishes a letter*) I had to change into me best. I can't stay.

CYNTHIA. What do you mean, you can't stay? (*She moves to Mrs D'Arcy*) What is that?

MRS D'ARCY. It's from Sir Robert Brunning, my plastic surgeon. He's going to do me nose at last.

CYNTHIA. But the sweep's here.

MRS D'ARCY. Yes, miss. I'm sorry, but I must go—I said I'd be free any time he could fit me in. (*She crosses to the fireplace*)

CYNTHIA (*handing the cup to Sarah*) You won't be at the hospital all day.

MRS D'ARCY. No. He says he only wants to look at my nose today. But you never can tell. Last time the dentist said that things was a bit slack and he whipped three teeth out. (*She examines her nose in the mirror over the fireplace*)

CYNTHIA (*picking up the newspaper from the sofa*) Do get back as soon as you can. (*She moves to* L *of the sofa*) Would you have time to take the tray before you go? (*She moves up* C *and puts the paper on the sideboard*)

MRS D'ARCY. Oh, yes, I'll have time for that. (*She sighs*) I only wish D'Arcy was here to see it when it's done. "Sheila," 'e used to say, "when the pools come up, we'll have that nose of yours ironed out." (*She crosses to the table and helps Sarah to stack the tray*) Does Mr Henry know Sir Robert Brunning? Do they work together?

SARAH (*moving* R) My brother's a psychiatrist.

MRS D'ARCY. Well, they all stick together, don't they, like plumbers and decorators. It's going to cost a hundred pounds or more. I tried the National Health but they wouldn't wear me. Like my 'at?

SARAH. Lovely. I thought you were off to Ascot.

MRS D'ARCY. No, not Ascot. It was for the Derby, nineteen-thirty-one. Take my tip, never throw an 'at away. (*She picks up the loaded tray, crosses and looks in the mirror*) Oh, dear, I do wish D'Arcy was alive to see me new nose, I'm sure 'e'd think his insurance money was well spent.

(MRS D'ARCY *exits to the kitchen.* SARAH *moves to the telephone and lifts the receiver*)

CYNTHIA. Who are you telephoning?

SARAH. Paul. I told him I might meet him for coffee.

CYNTHIA. If you want to make arrangements like that you should get up earlier.

SARAH (*replacing the receiver*) Now don't take it out on me because Mrs D'Arcy is having time off.

CYNTHIA (*moving below the sofa*) You seem to forget this is my holiday—I've done nothing but work.

SARAH (*crossing to* RC) Whose fault is that? No-one asked you to turn father's old study into mother's bedroom.

CYNTHIA. Henry thinks it's wrong for her to have her room right at the top of the house.

SARAH. Henry is like all psychiatrists, he's never happy until he has *something* wrong with everyone.

(HENRY WALLING *enters from the hall. He is in his thirties and is smartly but soberly dressed. He wears heavy, horn-rimmed spectacles, and carries a brief-case*)

I'm sure he invents half those complexes.

HENRY. I can assure you I don't, Sarah. Why is the front door open?

CYNTHIA. Mrs D'Arcy probably left it open for the sweep. Henry, why are you here so early?

HENRY. I'm having a little difficulty with one of my patients. She's run away.

SARAH (*crossing to the sideboard*) From you? (*She picks up her newspaper*)

CYNTHIA (*sharply*) Sarah! (*She moves* C) Who is she, Henry?

HENRY (*crossing to* R *of Cynthia*) Rosita Hernandez. The Araguyan Ambassador's stepdaughter.

CYNTHIA. What's the matter with her?

HENRY. She never got on with her stepfather. Given her very bad inhibitions. I could hardly get her on the couch at first—and now she's cured I couldn't get her off it. She tried to make me a substitute for her father.

SARAH. She must be in a bad way. (*She moves and sits on the upstage arm of the easy chair* L)

HENRY. That'll do, Sarah. I've made excellent headway with the girl. I can't understand what's gone wrong.

SARAH. Probably your diagnosis.

CYNTHIA. Why are you here?

HENRY. She's developed a dependence on me, so she may be coming here. If she does, let me know at once.

(CYNTHIA *moves to the table and folds the cloth.*
MRS D'ARCY *enters from the kitchen*)

MRS D'ARCY. Well, I'll be off, now, Miss Cynthia. (*She crosses to Henry*) Oh, Mr Henry—I'm just off to Sir Robert Brunning, 'e's going to do me nose. Do you know him?

HENRY. I have met him. He's very expensive, you know.

MRS D'ARCY. You're telling me. If I mention your name would there be a discount?

HENRY. I hardly think so. I don't know him well. (*He puts his brief-case on the table*) Has anyone called for me today or yesterday?

MRS D'ARCY. I don't know, sir. I've only just come.

(FLAHERTY *enters from the garden with his brushes*)

FLAHERTY (*to Henry*) Good day to you, sir. (*He glances at Mrs D'Arcy*) This will be the lady of the house? (*He does a slight "take" at Mrs D'Arcy's nose*)

MRS D'ARCY. I'm the housekeeper. (*She crosses to* R) Come this way. I'll be back as soon as I can, Miss Cynthia. And next time you see me, my nose'll be straighter than them brushes. I'm going to have it done.

FLAHERTY (*crossing to* R) The sooner the better.

(MRS D'ARCY *and* FLAHERTY *exit to the hall*)

HENRY. Is that the sweep?

SARAH (*rising*) Is that psychiatry—or did you guess from his brushes? (*She drops her paper into the easy chair* L *and moves above the sofa*)

CYNTHIA (*to Henry*) I'm having an electric fire put in mother's new room. I thought I'd have the chimney swept first.

HENRY. An excellent idea. Is the room finished?

CYNTHIA. We have to tidy up after the sweep. It should be ready when she comes home tomorrow.

SARAH (*turning over the papers in the drawer on the table behind the sofa*) Cynthia is throwing away father's old papers.

HENRY. Quite right. This clinging to the past is most unhealthy.

SARAH. Here's an old photograph of all of us.

(HENRY *moves to* R *of Sarah*)

I was rather an attractive baby. You look dreadful, Cynthia—your knickers are hanging down.

(CYNTHIA *puts the folded cloth on the table and moves to* R *of Henry*)

HENRY (*taking the photograph from Sarah*) I remember that. I got my cricket colours that year. First time I wore that blazer.

CYNTHIA. It was taken when we were evacuated. It must have been the year father was killed.

SARAH. Could I have it to show Paul?

CYNTHIA (*taking the photograph from Henry*) No, you could not. He's the last person to see it.

SARAH. He'd love to see you looking like that.

CYNTHIA. I'm sure he would, but he's not going to.

SARAH. I know you both hate Paul Martell but mother likes him. (*She moves to the fireplace*)

HENRY (*moving below the sofa*) I wouldn't call mother an astute judge of character. She spoils you, Sarah. The whole idea of letting you attend a drama school is ridiculous. All that has come out of it so far is that unemployed actor.

(FLAHERTY, *unnoticed by the others, appears at the hall door and leans on the jamb.* CYNTHIA *puts the photograph in the drawer*)

SARAH. He's writing a play. The time will come when Martell will be a household word.

HENRY. His name already is a household word. He's a typically uncouth adolescent. He's only interested in your money.

SARAH. My money! I haven't any.

HENRY (*loudly*) No, but mother has and the sooner he finds out it isn't yours, the better.

(CYNTHIA *picks up the drawer, turns and sees Flaherty*)

CYNTHIA. Sh! (*She puts the drawer on the table up* RC)

FLAHERTY (*coming easily into the room*) Don't mind me, miss. I'm from a big family meself. One of me sisters ran off with a tinker. What a shenanigans that caused. (*He crosses to the garden door*) Better get me sack. There might be a bit of soot.

CYNTHIA. You won't find any soot. The chimney hasn't been used for years.

FLAHERTY. I'll get me sack, all the same. Never know what ye'll find. Couple of dead cats up me last one.

(FLAHERTY *exits to the garden*)

HENRY (*to Sarah*) The money we spent on your education was completely wasted. You're ready to marry the first lout that looks at you.

SARAH. You've only met Paul once.

HENRY. That was enough. I'm trained to observe people, don't forget. His motives were very plain.

Sarah (*impassioned*) I can decide who I want to marry without being psychoanalysed. I don't care if my education is wasted—I don't care!

(Flaherty *enters from the garden carrying his sacks*)

Henry. Then you ought to be ashamed of yourself.

Cynthia (*seeing Flaherty*) Shhhh!

Flaherty. Don't be shushing them.

(Sarah *sits in the easy chair* L. Henry *crosses to the fireplace*)

Let them have their say. I mind me father saying he'd throw this tinker I'm speakin' of into the bog. The last time I seen them they was crackin' a bottle celebrating me sister's seventh son.

Cynthia (*crossing and putting the tablecloth on the sideboard*) Suppose you tell us about your family some other time, Mr Flaherty. I should like that chimney swept.

Flaherty (*crossing to the hall door*) Sure enough, it'll be done. I don't like to hear the young girl say education is wasted. It never is. I was head boy at a Christian Brother's school meself and I never regretted it. And how much better for you to have a feller like me for to sweep your chimney.

Henry. If you ever get round to it.

(Cynthia *transfers a tray of drinks from the sideboard to the table behind the sofa*)

Flaherty. Ye'll not know I've been in the room.

(Flaherty *exits to the hall*)

Henry (*crossing to* R) He's certainly never out of this one. (*To Sarah*) I'll deal with you later. I must get back.

(Flaherty *enters from the hall*)

(*To Flaherty*) What do you want now?

Flaherty (*crossing to Cynthia*) About the brush, ma'am.

Cynthia. What about it?

Flaherty. Will I give ye a shout when I think it's through?

Cynthia. No, thank you.

Flaherty. You must see the brush come through. Tell you what I'll do. When it ought to be through I'll stamp on the floor above—like this. (*He stamps violently*) That'll let you know.

(Flaherty *exits to the hall*)

Henry. Do you have to have a man like that to sweep the chimney?

Cynthia. He was all we could get at short notice.

Henry. I must get back. Miss Parker may have heard something about Rosita.

Cynthia. We'd better wash up, Sarah.

(SARAH *rises*)

We can't do anything upstairs until he's finished.

(*There is a thud from above. They all start*)

That brush *can't* be through yet.

HENRY. What the devil is that?

SARAH. There's the first dead cat.

CYNTHIA (*crossing to Henry*) Will you be here tomorrow?

HENRY. I don't know. I'd like to meet mother if I can. But there's this Hernandez business and I'm supposed to be taking Pamela down to Sussex—she's jumping there.

CYNTHIA. You must bring her to dinner next week. (*She crosses, collects the tablecloth from the sideboard and hands it to Sarah*)

SARAH. Yes, do. She needn't dismount—she can have her meals off the mantelpiece.

HENRY. If she does come, I sincerely hope you'll be out.

SARAH. If you give me due warning I'll make a point of it.

(SARAH *exits to the kitchen*)

HENRY. It's essential that mother sleeps in that room. She has a fixation about father's old study.

(*There is another thud from above*)

CYNTHIA. From the noise he's making there won't be any room left for her to sleep in. Good-bye, Henry.

HENRY. Good-bye, Cynthia.

(CYNTHIA *crosses and exits to the kitchen.* HENRY *collects his brief-case and moves to the hall door.*

FLAHERTY *enters from the hall. He looks shaken and carries a large, dusty, black and white shoe*)

What is it now? What's that?

FLAHERTY. A shoe.

HENRY. I can see that. Is it yours?

FLAHERTY. I'd say it was yours—'twas up your chimney. Come down and give me a crack on the head. (*He rubs his head*)

HENRY. No great damage seems to have been done.

FLAHERTY (*eyeing the drinks*) Me head's buzzing. I think it's the shock.

HENRY. Sit down. I'll get you a drink. (*He puts his brief-case on the right arm of the sofa, moves to the table behind the sofa and pours a whisky*)

FLAHERTY (*sitting in the easy chair* RC) John Jameson, please. Slap on me head it came, heel first. Will I put it on the floor?

HENRY. Put it where you like. (*He crosses to Flaherty with the drink*)

(FLAHERTY *puts the shoe on the floor and takes the drink*)

FLAHERTY. Thank you. (*He sniffs*) This isn't John Jameson.

Henry. It's Vat sixty-nine. I don't drink Irish whiskey.

Flaherty. You should. Aren't you havin' one? (*He drinks*)

Henry. I don't drink in the mornings, thank you.

Flaherty. You'll drink *this* morning.

Henry. If you're sure you're feeling better, I'll be on my way. I have an appointment elsewhere.

Flaherty. Ye have one with me first. (*He picks up the shoe*)

Henry. What are you talking about? You're not trying to hold me responsible for the injury.

Flaherty. I hadn't thought of it.

Henry. Don't. I'm a member of the medical profession.

Flaherty. Then this shoe should be right up your street, Mr Walling.

Henry (*impatiently*) What are you talking about? Oh, throw the damned thing away.

Flaherty. And what about the other one?

Henry. You mean there are two? Well, throw them both away. I don't know what all this fuss is about. (*He moves to* R *of the sofa*)

Flaherty. Ah, sure, the shoes is nothing. (*He rises*) It's what they was on. The other one isn't down yet.

Henry. What they were *on?*

Flaherty (*putting the shoe and his glass on the coffee-table*) I'll tell ye the way it was. I had me first length of brush up a few feet and —wham! There's a stoppage. I shoved a bit harder—no move. So I takes out the brush and sticks me hand up the flue. What do I see? Two shoes, on a ledge. While I was wavin' me flashlight one of them come crack on me skull. I takes another look and I see they was bein' worn.

Henry. Worn?

Flaherty. Indeed they were. One of them still is.

Henry. Worn—by whom?

Flaherty. There ye have me. And the feller who worn 'em won't be tellin' ye. For there's little enough left of him.

Henry. *Left* of him?

Flaherty. I'd say it was many years since he went up your chimney.

Henry. Are you trying to tell me there's someone up that chimney? Is this some sort of joke?

Flaherty. It was no joke for the feller up there.

Henry. A body—in *our* chimney?

Flaherty. It's there right enough. Will you take a look? (*He waves his flashlight*) I have my flashlight. (*He turns to the hall door*)

(Sarah *enters from the kitchen and moves down* L)

Henry. I—I suppose I'd better. (*He snatches the shoe from the coffee-table*) Don't leave that there!

Sarah (*moving below the sofa*) Good heavens, what's that?

Henry (*turning to Sarah*) Oh—it's—er—one of Mr Fogarty's.

FLAHERTY. "Flaherty!"

HENRY. Yes, yes, of course. Mr Flaherty was just—er—showing it to me.

SARAH (*moving to* L *of Henry*) What on earth for?

FLAHERTY. I found it up——

HENRY (*moving to Flaherty; quickly*) —stairs. (*He nudges Flaherty*) In his sack.

FLAHERTY (*falling in*) Ah, yes indeed, miss. I didn't know it was there. I've been asking Mr Walling what he thinks of it. You see that, Mr Walling, ye wouldn't get a shoe like that these days.

HENRY (*looking in horror at the shoe*) No. It's a very fine shoe indeed.

FLAHERTY (*taking the shoe from Henry*) If you're coming to view this little obstruction, we'd better go.

HENRY. Yes. Yes, of course.

SARAH. Have you found another dead cat?

HENRY. *No!*

FLAHERTY. It's something I thought Mr Walling might help me with. A little difficulty.

(HENRY *crosses to the hall door*)

SARAH (*moving to* L *of Flaherty*) I'll give Mr Flaherty a hand. We can manage.

HENRY. *No!* You stay here.

(HENRY *rushes out to the hall, dragging* FLAHERTY *with him.* SARAH *stares after them, aghast, then picks up Flaherty's glass.*
CYNTHIA *enters from the kitchen and crosses to Sarah*)

CYNTHIA. What *are* doing, Sarah?

SARAH (*crossing to* C) Henry's just gone rushing upstairs with the sweep.

CYNTHIA. *Henry* has? With the *sweep?* Don't be ridiculous!

SARAH. It's the truth, I tell you. They were tossing a large shoe back and forth. (*She waves the glass*) They've been drinking whisky, too.

CYNTHIA. Are you sure you haven't been drinking whisky? (*She takes the glass from Sarah*)

SARAH. It's the truth, I tell you. (*She crosses to the hall door*) I think something has gone wrong up there.

CYNTHIA (*putting the glass on the coffee-table*) Why didn't you go up? You know Henry is in a hurry.

SARAH. I offered to. He nearly shrieked the place down.

CYNTHIA. I can't see Henry wanting to help the sweep.

SARAH. I can't think what's come over him. He looked as though he'd jumped straight off his own consulting couch.

CYNTHIA (*crossing to the hall door*) Well, I'm going up to see what's the matter,

(Henry *enters from the hall, crosses to the table behind the sofa, pours himself a stiff drink, then moves below the sofa and sits on it, staring straight before him.* Cynthia *and* Sarah *watch him, fascinated*)

(*She crosses to* R *of the sofa*) What's the matter with you, Henry?

Sarah. *Was* there something up the chimney?

(Henry *takes a gulp*)

Henry. There was—(*he gulps*) some*one* up there.

Sarah (*moving* RC) You mean that Mr Flaherty was stuck up there?

Henry. No—not Flaherty.

Cynthia. Then *who?* Henry, what has come over you?

Henry. He—he's found a body up there.

Cynthia. A *body?* You mean a human body?

Henry. Yes. What's left of one.

Cynthia. Let's get this straight. You mean there's a dead body up *our* chimney?

(Henry *nods, rises, moves behind the sofa and pours another drink for himself*)

Henry. How did it *get* there? (*He moves and sits at the left end of the sofa, taking his drink and the bottle of whisky with him*)

Cynthia. Henry, are you sure there's no mistake about this?

Henry. I've seen it myself—with Flaherty's flashlight.

Cynthia. But how long has it been there?

(Flaherty *enters from the hall, carrying the shoe.* Sarah *and* Cynthia *stare at it.* Flaherty *crosses, picks up his glass and sits* R *of Henry on the sofa.* Henry *pours some whisky into Flaherty's glass*)

Henry. Years. It's nearly gone. One of its shoes fell on Mr Flaherty.

Flaherty. Did you tell them? (*He drinks*)

(Cynthia *crosses above the sofa to* L *of it*)

Henry. I had to.

(Sarah *moves to* R *of the sofa*)

Flaherty. I'd say it was best. (*He looks at his glass*) You should get some Highland Mist. What did you say this was?

Henry. Vat sixty-nine.

Flaherty (*savouring*) It's not bad, but I prefer Highland Mist if I can't get John Jameson. Good luck. (*He drinks*)

Henry. Cheers! (*He drinks*)

Cynthia (*taking the bottle from Henry*) Don't sit there like a pair of whisky tasters. (*She puts the bottle on the table behind the sofa*) What are we going to do? (*She moves to the fireplace*)

Sarah. Is—is it far up?

FLAHERTY (*holding the shoe about four feet from the ground*) About that high, I'd say, wouldn't you, Mr Walling?

(HENRY *nods dismally*)

SARAH. Is that it's shoe?

FLAHERTY. It is. (*He displays it airily*)

(SARAH *recoils*)

Size ten, I'd say, Mr Walling.

(HENRY *eyes the shoe with aversion*)

A fair-sized feller, he was.

CYNTHIA. What I can't understand is how could anyone be up our chimney without us knowing?

FLAHERTY. I knew a feller, Malachy Quigley, shot four Black and Tans and shoved 'em up the chimney—not a soul knew until one Christmas his grandson started pokin' about for Santa Claus.

SARAH (*sitting on the right arm of the sofa*) What's a Black and Tan?

FLAHERTY. A crowd of fellers Lloyd George sent . . .

CYNTHIA. Be quiet, Mr Flaherty! Henry, there must be some simple explanation.

HENRY. What—for instance?

CYNTHIA. A—a workman mending the slates fell down the chimney.

FLAHERTY. Houdini couldn't have got down that chimney, miss. Anything bigger than a leprechaun would have to go up—and it's no leprechaun, not with size ten black and white shoes. (*He looks admiringly at the shoe*)

CYNTHIA (*turning away*) Will you put that revolting shoe down?

HENRY. Mr Flaherty, it might be as well if you tidied up. I want to speak to my sisters.

(FLAHERTY *looks around at the others, then rises*)

FLAHERTY. Ah, sure, I know how it is. When little Patrick found the Tans up the chimney, they had a great family conference. (*He puts the shoe and his glass on the coffee-table*) They called in their uncle. A great feller he was—a Police Superintendent. Yes, indeed.

(FLAHERTY *exits to the hall*)

HENRY (*rising and putting his glass on the coffee-table*) You hear? That should be our next move.

SARAH (*rising*) To get Malachy Quigley's uncle?

HENRY. No! The police.

CYNTHIA (*turning*) Do you really think so, Henry?

HENRY. What else does one do when human remains are found?

SARAH (*crossing to the telephone*) I'd better ring them.

HENRY. No!

SARAH. What shall we do, then?

HENRY (*pacing up and down*) I must think—I must *think.*

(*The telephone rings. They all start.* SARAH *lifts the receiver*)

SARAH (*into the telephone*) Heath three-o-four-nine . . . Oh, hullo, Paul . . . We're in a terrible flap here . . . We've found someone up the chimney . . .

(HENRY *and* CYNTHIA *rush to Sarah.* HENRY *slaps his hand over the mouthpiece*)

HENRY. You idiot! Get rid of him!

SARAH. Why—what did I say?

HENRY. You almost told him what we'd found. Say you'll call back.

SARAH (*into the telephone*) Sorry, Paul . . . No, I can't come to lunch . . . We've got the sweep here. I'll call you back. (*She replaces the receiver*)

HENRY. Haven't you a grain of sense? Do you have to tell everyone?

SARAH. They'll have to know sooner or later.

HENRY. Have they?

CYNTHIA. You mean—don't tell the police?

HENRY (*crossing to* L) Once they find out it will be in every newspaper in the country. I can see the headlines now. "Well-known psychiatrist finds body up chimney." I shall be ruined.

SARAH. Oh, I don't know. You might get more patients.

CYNTHIA (*crossing to* C) My chances of a Headship wouldn't be improved.

HENRY. Exactly! Who's going to trust children to a woman who took up two columns in the *News of the World?*

SARAH. She'd have to do a lot more than that to get *two* columns.

HENRY. Be quiet, Sarah.

(SARAH *moves up* C)

CYNTHIA. We can't just ignore it, Henry.

HENRY. I look at it this way. Whoever it is can't be missed. He's been there for years. (*He sits on the sofa*) A few days while we think things out can't make any difference.

SARAH. What about Mr Flaherty? I can just see him telling the owners of the next twenty chimneys he sweeps what he found up ours. (*She moves and sits on the left arm of the sofa*)

CYNTHIA. That's a point.

HENRY. I'll deal with Flaherty. A pound note and he'll forget all about it.

CYNTHIA. You think so.

HENRY. You leave him to me. Now, for the time being we tell *no-one.* Is that plain, Sarah?

SARAH. Why pick on me?

HENRY. Because you've already half told that Martell youth.

(FLAHERTY *enters from the hall, carrying his brushes*)

FLAHERTY. I've tidied up and left the asbestos sheet against the fireplace. (*He moves to the garden door*)

CYNTHIA (*crossing and closing the hall door*) Thank you very much.

FLAHERTY. Of course, your chimney's not swept. (*He puts his brushes outside the garden door*) But then the police won't want anything disturbed.

(*There is an awkward silence*)

Before I'm on me way, could I just have a drop of that Vat sixty-nine?

HENRY (*rising; eagerly*) Yes. There's no hurry, is there, Cynthia? I'll get it for you. (*He collects Flaherty's glass from the coffee-table, moves above the sofa and pours a whisky*)

CYNTHIA. Do sit down, Mr Flaherty. (*She moves the chair* R *of the table and sets it* C)

FLAHERTY (*sitting* C) Thank you.

CYNTHIA (*moving* R) I think now would be a good time for Mr Flaherty to tell us about his sister that ran off with a tailor.

(HENRY *takes the drink to Flaherty*)

FLAHERTY. A tinker it was. (*He takes the glass from Henry*) Thanks. (*He raises the glass*) Here's to himself above, God rest him. (*He drinks then puts his glass on the coffee-table*)

(CYNTHIA *sits on the right arm of the easy chair* RC. SARAH *sits on the sofa and puts her feet up.* HENRY *stands* L *of Flaherty*)

Ah, well, he was a clever feller this tinker. Sean Plunkett was his name. 'Twas him put me on to the *New Statesman.* He won a competition once. Ah, reminds me. (*He puts on his spectacles and takes out his newspaper*) I made a few notes for this week's competition.

HENRY. Mr Flaherty . . .

FLAHERTY. No. It's Sir Alfred Munning's foreword. It's my own composition. (*He reads*) "Visitors to the Picasso Exhibition are asked to empty their pockets at the entrance as the management cannot be responsible for any articles lost when they stand on their heads to look at the pictures." (*He looks around for approval*)

(*The others smile feebly*)

I'll tidy it a bit, of course. Oh, by the way, the police will want me address.

HENRY. Mr Flaherty, we were—er—thinking of not mentioning this to the police. (*He pauses*) Not for the moment, that is.

FLAHERTY. Were you not?

HENRY. We have been talking things over, and we've come to the conclusion that no useful purpose would be served by calling in the police—at this stage.

FLAHERTY (*blandly*) At what other stage would you call them? They don't like to be left out of these things for long. They'd raise hell if ye didn't call 'em at once.

HENRY. We could always pretend that we have only just discovered the—er—remains.

FLAHERTY. Ye could, except they might wonder what the blazes you were doing half-way up the chimney.

SARAH. We could say we heard a bird up there.

HENRY. Yes. No, you see, people in our position can't afford any unpleasant publicity.

FLAHERTY (*knowingly*) Ah, sure. Ye'd like to have a poke around the family first before you tell the police. Malachy had the same idea.

CYNTHIA (*rising*) You don't think that this body has anything to do with us? (*She crosses above the sofa to* L *of it*)

FLAHERTY. Well, 'tis up *your* chimney, miss.

HENRY. Yes, but we're quite confident that there's some simple explanation.

FLAHERTY. Y'are? I'd like to know what the hell it is, then.

SARAH. So should we.

HENRY. We don't *know* what. That's why we'd like a little time. Meanwhile, we'd be grateful if you'd keep what you found to yourself. After all, it might not do your business any good.

FLAHERTY. To tell the truth I was thinkin' of having an advertisement done—American style—"Flaherty gets *everything* out of your chimney—but *everything!*"

(SARAH *giggles*)

HENRY. It wouldn't do, I can assure you. Another thing—my mother will be home from Scotland tomorrow. We must warn her before the police come.

FLAHERTY (*confidentially*) I get you—give her a chance to skip off if she knows anything.

CYNTHIA (*indignantly*) Certainly not! We want to break it to her gently.

HENRY. If she found her home full of police and reporters the shock would probably kill her.

FLAHERTY (*rising and crossing to the hall door*) I'd better be fixing that asbestos back again.

HENRY (*with a look of triumph at Cynthia*) That's very kind of you. We appreciate it.

(CYNTHIA *moves to the fireplace*)

(*He replaces the chair at the table*) Don't worry, I'll see you don't lose by it.

FLAHERTY. I only hope it's the right thing I'm doing.

CYNTHIA. Of course it is. We'll tell the police you understood we were going to report it at once.

HENRY. Another whisky, Mr Flaherty? (*He moves above the sofa*) We must get some John Jameson, Cynthia.

FLAHERTY. I won't take another drop. I'll get the job done first. Keep an eye on me brushes.

HENRY. Of course. (*Importantly*) Cynthia, keep an eye on Mr Flaherty's brushes. (*To Flaherty*) Can I help you?

FLAHERTY. Not at all. It'll have to be done gentle. I don't want that other bloody shoe on me napper.

(FLAHERTY *exits to the hall*)

HENRY. There, I told you he'd be easy to manage. I'm not usually far out in my judgement of human nature.

CYNTHIA. Should we telephone mother and tell her to stay on for a day or two?

HENRY. No. She'll wonder why. We must try to carry on as normally as possible. Do you hear, Sarah?

(SARAH *is staring thoughtfully before her*)

(*He moves to* R *of Sarah*) Sarah! What's the matter?

SARAH. I was thinking about mother. (*She puts her feet down*)

HENRY. Well?

SARAH. She's lived in this house all her life. She might know who's up there. You're always saying she's emotionally unstable. Could she've put it up there herself?

HENRY. I never said she was a paranoic.

CYNTHIA. I don't think we should discuss this with mother.

SARAH. We'll have to—the body's in her bedroom.

CYNTHIA. Henry. I think you'd better meet her.

HENRY (*moving* R) Perhaps I will, before I collect Pamela. (*He stops, horrified*) Pamela! Our engagement's going to be announced in *The Times* on Monday. She must never know about this.

CYNTHIA (*crossing to* RC) No, you can't bring her to dinner next week.

SARAH (*rising*) If you do, make her leave her horse outside—too much stamping will bring the other shoe down.

HENRY (*crossing to* C) Will you stop your damned silly remarks! Use what little brain you have.

SARAH. I'm the only one who *is* thinking. All you and Cynthia are wondering is what people will say. I'm wondering who it is.

HENRY. How could we know who it is?

(CYNTHIA *crosses to* R)

SARAH. Cast your mind back. Has anyone in the family disappeared, say twenty years ago?

(*There is a moment's silence.* HENRY *and* CYNTHIA *look at each other, aghast*)

HENRY. You don't mean—father?

Cynthia. He was killed in an air-raid.

Sarah. Well, that's what mother tells everyone.

Henry. Yes, I had to stop her from telling Pamela it was at that terrible night-club.

Sarah (*moving to* L *of Henry*) What are you going to tell the Honourable Pamela now—that he was blown up the flue? (*She moves to the kitchen door*)

Henry. I refuse to believe that man up that chimney is my father. He was a solicitor—he wouldn't have worn those—those co-respondent's shoes.

Cynthia. Perhaps he used them for some kind of sport.

Sarah. Perhaps he *did.* I'm going to make some coffee.

(Sarah *exits to the kitchen.*
Flaherty *enters from the hall*)

Flaherty. I think that'll be fine, now. Take a look at it. You wouldn't know I'd been there. (*He collects his glass, crosses to the table behind the sofa and pours himself a drink*)

(Henry *looks hesitantly at Cynthia*)

Ah, sure, take her.

Henry. What?

Flaherty. I'd like her to see it. I only hope when me time comes someone makes as neat a job of coverin' me up.

(Henry *and* Cynthia *exit to the hall.* Flaherty *looks at the shoe, then reclines on the sofa with his drink, and reads his newspaper.*
Paul Martell *enters from the garden. He is an unconventionally dressed young man in his early twenties*)

Paul. Anyone here?

Flaherty (*peering over the back of the sofa*) Just meself.

Paul (*moving to* R *of the sofa*) Where is Sarah?

Flaherty. She's about somewhere. Are you the young feller her brother was givin' her hell about? You don't look so bad to me.

Paul. Well, thank you. Is there any point in asking who you are?

Flaherty. Flaherty. Dermot Ignatius Eamon McMorragh Flaherty. Descended, as you may well guess, from the Kings of Ireland. I came to sweep the chimney.

Paul. What's this—a tea break?

Flaherty. Well, y'see, we ran into a bit of trouble.

Paul. Ah, yes. Sarah said you got stuck up the chimney.

Flaherty. *Me!*

Paul. I presume it was you. (*He moves down* RC) I can't see Henry or Cynthia up one.

Flaherty. Ah, sure, you're right there, boy. Well, it's down I am again now.

(Sarah *enters from the kitchen, carrying a cup of coffee*)

SARAH (*crossing to Paul*) Paul! How did you get in?

PAUL. The side gate was open—are you coming out for coffee?

SARAH. No, Paul. Do go. Henry will be furious if he finds you here.

FLAHERTY. Is that a cup of tea you've got there?

SARAH. No, coffee. But I can make you some tea if you like, Mr Flaherty.

FLAHERTY. No matter. Do you have a sandwich?

(PAUL *watches with growing amazement*)

SARAH. Would you like chicken?

FLAHERTY. That'll be all right. Cut the crust off, the teeth aren't what they were.

PAUL (*heavily*) Any particular kind of bread?

FLAHERTY. Wholemeal, if you please. (*He reads*)

SARAH. I'll say good-bye to Paul first.

PAUL (*determinedly*) Now, listen to me! (*He takes the coffee from Sarah, puts it on the coffee-table and sees the shoe*) What's that? (*He picks up the shoe*)

SARAH (*snatching the shoe*) You can't have that. (*She tosses the shoe on to the floor by the sideboard*)

FLAHERTY. 'Tis Mr Walling's.

SARAH (*crossing to the fireplace*) It belongs to—to an old friend.

FLAHERTY. A very old friend.

PAUL. Who?

SARAH (*moving to* L *of the sofa*) A friend of mother's. He hasn't been here for years.

PAUL (*heavily*) I see—and the last time he called he left his shoes behind.

FLAHERTY. Among other things.

SARAH. So mother kept them—in case he ever came back.

FLAHERTY (*rising*) Look, dear, don't bother about the sandwiches. I'll collect me brushes. (*He moves up* C, *picks up the shoe and puts it on the table*) I wouldn't throw that shoe away—the police may like to see it eventually.

(FLAHERTY *exits to the garden, taking his brushes with him*)

PAUL (*crossing to* R *of Sarah*) The police? What would they want with it?

SARAH. Oh! He—he thinks they might call about—about that friend of mother's. If he's missing, you see.

PAUL. I'm damned if I do. Kiss me.

SARAH. No. I haven't time.

PAUL. Haven't time! You have enough time for the sweep. What's the matter with you?

SARAH. He's helping us. Paul, you must go. (*She drags Paul up* C) I'll see you at the week-end.

PAUL. You promise?

Sarah. Yes.

Paul. All right, I'm going.

(Sarah *gives Paul a hasty peck.* Paul *grabs her and it becomes quite a lingering affair.*

Henry *and* Cynthia *enter from the hall. They look aghast at Paul and Sarah*)

Henry. Sarah! Have you taken leave of your senses?

(Sarah, *a little dazed, breaks from Paul and moves below the sofa*)

Sarah. Oh—Henry. You—know Paul Martell.

Henry. I do, and I have no wish to extend the acquaintance.

Paul. Now look here, Walling . . .

Henry (*crossing down* L; *icily*) We have family matters to discuss, Mr Martell. Will you excuse us—you can leave through the side gate.

Sarah. Henry, don't you dare talk to Paul like that.

Cynthia. Mr Martell, you heard what my brother said. We have family . . .

Paul (*interrupting*) I heard you the first time. Don't get on your high horses with me, the pair of you. Just because someone got stuck up your damned chimney.

(Henry *and* Cynthia *look at each other, aghast*)

Henry. W-what did you say? Sarah, what have you told him?

Sarah. I—I haven't told him anything, he must have been talking to Flaherty.

Henry. My God! The babbler! (*He moves to* L *of Paul. With a forced smile*) Now—look here, Paul, old man . . .

Paul (*slightly apprehensive*) Eh?

Henry. Do you really have to go? (*He puts his arm around Paul and leads him to the easy chair* RC) Sit down, old chap. How about a cigar?

Paul (*sitting gingerly in the easy chair* RC) Well—thanks.

Henry (*moving to the table behind the sofa*) Drink?

Paul. Well—er—yes. I don't mind if I do.

Henry (*with forced heartiness*) Sherry or Vat sixty-nine? (*He waves the bottle*)

Paul. Vat sixty-nine.

Henry (*pouring a drink for Paul*) I won't offer you any Martell.

Cynthia (*swallowing her pride*) You mustn't take much notice of Mr Flaherty. You know how these Celts exaggerate.

Henry (*handing the drink to Paul*) Yes—as a matter of fact I've just looked up the chimney myself.

Paul (*edgily*) You—you have? (*He drinks*)

Cynthia. Yes, he has.

Henry. Yes, I have—with Flaherty's flashlight. You must take anything he tells you with a grain of salt.

Cynthia. Yes, you must.

PAUL (*bewildered*) Yes. Yes, I will.

HENRY (*after a pause*) Well, that's settled. It's nice to see you again. We're delighted to see Sarah mixing with such reliable young people, aren't we, Cynthia?

CYNTHIA (*crossing above the sofa*) Eh? Oh, yes, we are. Yes, Henry.

HENRY. Another drink? (*He takes Paul's glass*) You must come round more often. Any time. (*He pours another drink for Paul*)

CYNTHIA (*moving to the fireplace*) Yes, any time.

SARAH (*sitting on the sofa*) Oh, yes, any time.

(FLAHERTY *enters from the garden*)

FLAHERTY (*seeing the glass in Henry's hand*) That for me?

HENRY (*a little put out*) No. (*He crosses and hands the drink to Paul*) As a matter of fact it's for our young friend here—Mr—Paul . . .

FLAHERTY. Hello there, young feller.

PAUL. Well, I must say you don't look any worse for being stuck up the flue. I suppose it's happened to you before?

FLAHERTY. Not at all. Me first time ever.

HENRY (*alert*) You told this young man that *you* were stuck up there?

FLAHERTY (*winking*) Wasn't it the truth? We must admit our errors, Mr Walling.

(HENRY *turns to Paul and takes the drink from him*)

HENRY. As I was saying, Mr Martell, we've family matters to discuss.

(PAUL *rises, shattered by* HENRY'S *change of manner.* FLAHERTY *takes the glass from Henry, crosses down* L *and drinks*)

(*He takes Paul by the arm and bustles him to the garden door*) If you'll excuse us.

SARAH (*rising*) Henry—what are you doing?

CYNTHIA. Be quiet, Sarah.

PAUL. Now, look here . . .

HENRY. Some other time, if you don't mind.

PAUL. Well, of all the . . .

HENRY. That'll do.

PAUL (*suddenly angry*) I don't know what's wrong with your patients, but *you're* barmy.

(PAUL *glares at everyone, including Sarah and storms out by the garden door*)

SARAH (*running to the garden door*) What have you done? He'll *never* come back.

(SARAH *exits to the garden*)

HENRY. That's fine. (*To Flaherty*) I misjudged you for a moment,

Mr Flaherty. That's a fine job you've made of that fireplace. Will you have one more before you go?

FLAHERTY. If you insist. (*He hands the glass to Cynthia*)

(CYNTHIA *hands the glass to* HENRY *who refills it*)

CYNTHIA. Do sit down, Mr Flaherty.

FLAHERTY (*crossing to* C) If I sit down, I'll never get up. No, I must go. I have the flue to clean out at the bakery.

(HENRY *hands the drink to Flaherty.*
SARAH *enters from the garden*)

(*He raises his glass*) To himself above there. (*He drinks*)

SARAH. You attend the bakery?

FLAHERTY. Yes. I leave that job till last—when I can—it makes a change going home all white. (*He hands his empty glass to Sarah*)

(SARAH *puts the glass on the sideboard, then crosses and sits in the easy chair* L)

HENRY (*taking out his wallet*) Now, Mr Flaherty, I want to give you something . . .

FLAHERTY. You can put that away. (*He sits in the easy chair* RC)

CYNTHIA. Oh, no—we insist. (*She sits on the sofa*)

HENRY. We certainly do.

FLAHERTY. Well, I'll tell ye what ye can do then. It's a great reader I am. Anything I like to read. Only the other day I was readin' about them parallel lines of Einstein's. Read a bit of psychiatry, too—your line, Mr W.

HENRY. You have? We must have a little talk about it one of these days.

FLAHERTY. We shall. We shall. We'll have many talks, I'm sure. To tell the truth, I'm after seein' a feller tonight about the *Encyclopaedia Brittanica.*

HENRY. Really? A fine work.

FLAHERTY. It is indeed. This feller wants me to buy it. Ye put so much down and go on paying and paying for years to come.

CYNTHIA. I don't really approve of hire-purchase.

FLAHERTY. Me own thought exactly. Don't like it at all. You pay far too much in the long run. So now I'm thinking that with your help I might slap down the money and buy it outright.

HENRY. What?

FLAHERTY. Ye needn't pay me until I've been into it with this feller. I'll be around tomorrow. (*He rises and moves up* C)

HENRY. Just a minute. How much is it?

FLAHERTY. Well, the edition that catches me eye is one in Moroccan leather. As the man says to me, "Mr Flaherty, you are buyin' a university—why not have a well-bound one?" It's about a hundred and eighty guineas. As it's between friends—I'll take a cheque.

HENRY. But that's black . . .

(*The others look aghast at Flaherty*)

FLAHERTY. That figure, of course, includes sweepin' the rest of your chimneys.

FLAHERTY *gives them a benevolent smile and exits to the garden as—*

the CURTAIN *falls*

ACT II

SCENE—*The same. The next morning.*

When the CURTAIN *rises,* SARAH *is lying on the sofa, reading a magazine. She has her transistor radio playing beside her. There is a knock at the front door.*

SARAH (*calling*) Mrs D'Arcy, Mrs D'Arcy, that'll be mother. (*She switches off the transistor and rises*)

(MRS D'ARCY *enters from the kitchen*)

MRS D'ARCY. No, miss, it's the delivery van. I've seen it from upstairs.

SARAH. Oh.

(*Two thuds are heard off* R)

What is going on there, Mrs D'Arcy?

(MRS D'ARCY *crosses and exits to the hall.*

PAUL *enters from the hall carrying a heavy carton which he puts on the floor down* R)

Paul, did you bring that?

(MRS D'ARCY *enters from the hall*)

MRS D'ARCY. There's three big boxes for Mr Henry.

PAUL. Yes. I was waiting on the doorstep when the delivery man brought them.

MRS D'ARCY. He never told you what they was, did he?

PAUL. No, I signed for them, though.

MRS D'ARCY. Oh, dear, I only hope there's nothing unpleasant in them. (*She crosses to the kitchen door*) Doctors have some funny things in bottles—livers and that. Sir Robert says there's no reason why me nose shouldn't be Grecian. What's that?

PAUL. Helen of Troy.

MRS D'ARCY. Not likely! I've heard about 'er!

(MRS D'ARCY *exits to the kitchen*)

SARAH. You can't stay, Paul.

PAUL (*moving to her*) Why not?

SARAH. Cynthia's having a bath.

PAUL. So? I wasn't planning on joining her. I just wondered if there was any chance of our lunching together?

SARAH. Well, I don't see why not. I'll just say hello to mother, and meet you at the club. Henry's gone to meet her.

Paul. How long will that be?

Sarah. They should be here any minute. I thought you were Henry.

Paul. That screwball!

Sarah. Darling—don't be so aggressive. Promise me next time you see them you'll be polite to them. You'll see, you'll grow on them.

Paul. If I can get a word in edgeways.

Cynthia (*off* R) What is all this?

Sarah. Oh, that's Cynthia. Paul, you can't stay. You can see mother at the weekend. (*She draws Paul up* C)

(Cynthia, *looking displeased, enters from the hall*)

Cynthia. What are those boxes doing in the hall? (*She sees the carton down* R) There's one here, too.

Sarah. Paul brought it in.

Cynthia. Then he can take it out again.

Paul (*loudly*) Now, look here . . .

Sarah (*quickly*) They belong to Henry, Cynthia.

Cynthia. Then it would have been better to leave them in the hall. Kindly take them outside again, Mr Martell. (*She moves up* RC)

(Paul *opens his mouth to speak.* Sarah *looks appealingly at him.* Paul *takes a deep breath, crosses, picks up the carton and exits to the hall*)

(*She moves to* R *of Sarah*) What's *he* doing here?

Sarah. He's taking me out to lunch.

Cynthia. Don't be ridiculous. You can't go now—with all this hanging over us.

Sarah. Why not!

(Mrs D'Arcy *enters from the kitchen carrying some clean towels*)

Cynthia (*seeing Mrs D'Arcy*) Ssh!

Mrs D'Arcy (*crossing to the hall door*) That Sir Robert's such a gentleman. My nose couldn't have been treated better if it had been on a duchess.

(Paul *enters from the hall carrying a delivery note*)

Paul. This came with the boxes. It's a delivery note.

(Paul *hands the note to Mrs D'Arcy and exits to the hall*)

Mrs D'Arcy (*looking at the note*) 'Ullo. (*She reads*) "Dermot Ignatius Eamon McMorragh Flaherty." Who are they?

(Cynthia *and* Sarah *react violently*)

Cynthia. They're the sweep.

Mrs D'Arcy. What, all of them?

Sarah. They belong to that sweep.

Cynthia (*moving to* L *of Mrs D'Arcy*) Yes. No. Mrs D'Arcy, he's coming again to see Mr Henry. (*She takes the note from Mrs D'Arcy*)

Mrs D'Arcy. Mr Henry? What does he want to see him for?

Cynthia. He's going to treat Mr Flaherty.

Sarah. What!

Mrs D'Arcy. You mean that sweep's round the bend? He looks all right to me.

Cynthia. Oh, he looks all right to us, but Mr Henry's trained to observe these things.

Mrs D'Arcy. 'Ere, what's in them boxes?

Sarah. Full of instruments to treat Mr Flaherty.

Mrs D'Arcy. I get you. Mr Henry's going to get him on the couch. I expect he's got some things in there to tie him down and poke his brains about. I've seen how they do it on the telly.

(Mrs D'Arcy *exits to the hall*)

Cynthia. What the blazes does that man Flaherty mean sending all his stuff here?

Sarah (*crossing to Cynthia*) Perhaps he's moving in.

Cynthia (*crossing and putting the note on the table behind the sofa*) What! Then he can move out. (*She calls*) Mr Martell.

Paul (*off*) Yes?

(Paul *enters from the hall*)

Cynthia. Kindly take those boxes into the garden.

Paul. Eh?

Cynthia. Through the windows. (*She moves to the fireplace*)

Paul (*outraged*) I'll be d——

(Sarah *looks appealingly at Paul*)

—delighted.

(Paul *exits thunderously to the hall*)

Sarah (*crossing to Cynthia*) You can't talk to Paul like that. He doesn't work here.

Cynthia. He does this morning. What can that man be thinking of, having all that stuff sent here?

(Paul *enters from the hall carrying three cartons*)

Paul (*crossing to the garden door*) What has Henry got in here—disused patients?

Sarah. Can I help you?

Paul. No.

(Paul *exits to the garden*)

Sarah (*moving* C) Why do you keep moving them about?

Cynthia (*sitting on the sofa*) They must be out of sight before mother comes. She'll want to know who they're for.

SARAH. Oh, yes, of course. (*She sits on the right arm of the sofa*)

(MRS D'ARCY *enters from the hall*)

MRS D'ARCY. 'Ere—those boxes have gone.
CYNTHIA. Yes. It's all right, Mrs D'Arcy. I want them in the garden.
MRS D'ARCY. In the garden?
CYNTHIA. They need to be kept fresh.
MRS D'ARCY. Kept *fresh?*

(PAUL *enters from the garden and throws himself on to the chair* L *of the table*)

PAUL. Oh!

(*The front door is heard to slam*)

MRS D'ARCY. Oh, here they are.

(MRS D'ARCY *exits to the hall*. CYNTHIA *rises*. SARAH *rises, moves to* PAUL *and pulls him to his feet*)

SARAH. That'll be mother—you can't stay. I'll show you out.
PAUL. What is this—Henry's private nut-house?

(SARAH *and* PAUL *exit to the garden*)

SYBIL (*off*) No, Henry. Those have to go upstairs.
HENRY (*off*) All right, Mother.

(SYBIL WALLING *enters from the hall. She is in her early sixties, smartly dressed, but has an air of vagueness which makes her seem a little older than she looks at first glance.* CYNTHIA *crosses to Sybil*)

SYBIL (*crossing to* RC) Cynthia dear. (*She kisses Cynthia*)
CYNTHIA. Hello, Mother. Have a good time?

(MRS D'ARCY *enters from the hall*)

SYBIL. Wonderful! How are you, Mrs D'Arcy? Everything all right?
MRS D'ARCY. Fine, ma'am. Oh, I've got such . . .
CYNTHIA. Help Mr Henry with the bags, will you, Mrs D'Arcy?
MRS D'ARCY. Right. You can tell her about me operation.

(MRS D'ARCY *exits to the hall*)

SYBIL (*crossing to* LC) Is she ill?
CYNTHIA. No. It's her nose. She's having it altered at last.
SYBIL. I'm so glad. Every morning I hate it. By the end of the day I'm used to it, but next morning I have to start all over again. Whenever I don't see her for a while I think to myself, it can't be as big as *that;* then when I do see her it's even bigger.
CYNTHIA (*moving to* R *of the sofa*) You must be tired. Have you had lunch?

SYBIL. Yes. With Henry. (*She moves to the fireplace*) I'm not tired, I had a sleeper. You know how I hate travelling—but a sleeper makes all the difference. I drop off to sleep and when I wake up I'm nearly there. I like to put things out of my mind, then I can think they're not. Like Mrs D'Arcy's nose.

CYNTHIA (*moving down* C) Yes.

SYBIL. I know I'm an ostrich but it's better to be like that, then all sorts of unpleasant things can be pushed out of sight.

(CYNTHIA *looks apprehensively at Sybil and sits in the easy chair* RC)

Well, has anything happened while I've been away? (*She crosses to* C)

CYNTHIA. N-no, Mother. Why should anything have happened?

SYBIL. I don't know. Things do happen, don't they? Has Pamela been, or that nice young man of Sarah's?

CYNTHIA. Oh, yes, that sort of thing has been happening.

(SYBIL *crosses towards the hall door*)

(*She rises and intercepts Sybil*) Where are you going, Mother?

SYBIL. Up to my room.

CYNTHIA (*aghast*) You can't. It's not there.

SYBIL. What?

CYNTHIA. I mean, we've moved your bedroom into father's old study.

SYBIL. You want me to sleep in father's old study? What made you do that?

CYNTHIA. Darling, we thought it would be better for you. Not so many stairs.

(SYBIL *moves to the sofa*)

You don't like the idea?

SYBIL. I—I'm not sure, dear. It's all rather unexpected. (*Thoughtfully*) I suppose there's no reason why I shouldn't sleep there. (*She sits on the sofa, at the right end of it*)

CYNTHIA (*moving to* R *of the sofa*) Yes, there is.

SYBIL. Cynthia, what *is* the matter with you?

CYNTHIA (*crossing to the fireplace*) I mean, it's not finished yet—you'll have to use the spare room for a day or two.

SYBIL. I see. What's the matter with Henry?

CYNTHIA (*turning to Sybil*) Henry?

SYBIL. He said he wanted to have a little talk with me. Then all through luncheon he never said a word. I watched him looking at me—as though I were one of his patients. Then when I caught him, he'd look down very quickly at his salad. The last time he behaved like that was when I caught him putting newts in the bath.

CYNTHIA. He's worried.

SYBIL. About Pamela? Oh, have they had an argument? Oh, dear. She is such an aloof girl. Whenever I want to speak to her, I always feel as though I ought to raise my hand.

CYNTHIA. No. He has a difficult case. A South American Ambassador's stepdaughter.

SYBIL. I don't care for South Americans. They steal girls out of cinemas.

(HENRY *enters from the hall and stands staring at Sybil.* SYBIL *looks up quickly.* HENRY *straightens his tie*)

HENRY. Ah.

SYBIL. Henry dear! Do stop staring at me like that. What's the matter with you?

CYNTHIA (*moving to* L *of Sybil*) He's glad to see you back. We—we all are. (*She moves to the kitchen door*) I'll go and make some coffee for you.

SYBIL. Thank you, dear.

(CYNTHIA *gives Henry a significant glance and exits quickly to the kitchen*)

HENRY (*moving* C) Have a nice time with Mrs McDonald, Mother?

SYBIL. You've asked me that seven times. Yes, I did.

HENRY. Good. Glad to be home?

SYBIL. Of course. Cynthia tells me she's turned father's old study into a bedroom for me.

HENRY (*crossing to the fireplace*) Yes. Much better. No stairs, or not so many. Blood-pressure, you know.

SYBIL. I don't have blood-pressure.

HENRY. No—now I don't suppose you ever will.

(SARAH *enters from the garden*)

SARAH (*running to Sybil*) Mummy.

SYBIL. Hello, dear. (*She kisses Sarah*)

SARAH. Have a nice time with Mrs McDonald?

SYBIL. Ask Henry. How are you, Sarah?

SARAH (*sitting in the easy chair* RC) Oh, fine, fine.

SYBIL. How is that bright young friend of yours—Paul?

SARAH. He's fine, too. He'll be here at the week-end.

HENRY. Sarah! (*He crosses to* L *of Sarah*) You can't have him here under the circumstances.

SYBIL. What circumstances? Why shouldn't he come? I like him.

HENRY. I'll explain later, Mother dear. Sarah knows what I mean.

SYBIL (*rising*) I shall go upstairs to one or the other of my rooms. (*She crosses to the hall door*) Perhaps by the time I come down you'll be more normal, Henry. You're behaving in a most peculiar manner.

(SYBIL *exits to the hall*)

SARAH (*rising*) Well, did you find out anything?

Henry. We've only just arrived, haven't we? I shall raise the matter at a favourable moment. It's all very difficult. I was wondering if . . .

Sarah (*crossing to the sofa*) It couldn't be one of the men who built the house? He fell asleep and they built the chimney round him—they worked a lot quicker in those days.

Henry. Don't chatter, Sarah—I'm thinking.

Sarah (*sitting on the sofa*) About Flaherty?

Henry. The man is nothing more than a common blackmailer. I've no room for a man like that.

Sarah. You'd better make room for him. His things are outside in the garden.

Henry. What?

Sarah. A lot of them. (*She rises and collects the delivery note from the table behind the sofa*) They arrived this morning. (*She hands the note to Henry*) He looks as if he's coming for a long stay.

Henry. The infernal impudence! I—I—I'd like to stuff him up a chimney.

Sarah. Not here—we're too crowded.

Henry. Cheek of it! (*He reads the note*) "Dermot Ignatius Eamon . . ."

Sarah. We've had all that.

Henry. "Care of Henry Walling, Esquire." (*He moves* R) He hasn't even put my letters after my name.

(Cynthia *enters from the kitchen.* Sarah *sits in the easy chair down* L)

Cynthia (*crossing to Henry*) Oh, Henry. Forgot to tell you. Miss Parker telephoned. Rosita Hernandez is still missing.

Henry. Damn Rosita Hernandez! Have you seen this? (*He shows the note to Cynthia*)

Cynthia. Yes, it's Mr Flaherty's.

Henry. It's too bad. It's gone much too far. He hasn't been here, has he? (*He puts the note on the dining-table up* R)

Cynthia. No. But I've prepared the ground. I told Mrs D'Arcy he was coming to consult you—as a patient.

Henry. What on earth made you say that?

Sarah. I think it's a brilliant idea. If he comes while mother's around we'll tell her the same thing, then it won't matter if Flaherty does come and live with us.

Henry. I refuse to live in the same house with him.

Sarah. He'll probably be sharing your room.

Henry. *Sarah!*

Cynthia. Where is mother?

Henry. Upstairs. Good grief! Father's study.

Cynthia (*calmly*) It's all right. I've locked it. (*Not so calmly*) The key. What have I done with it? (*She crosses to the fireplace and takes the key from the mantelpiece*) Ah, here it is.

HENRY (*crossing to Cynthia*) I'll take that then it can be lost. (*He takes the key from Cynthia*)

CYNTHIA. By the way, she doesn't seem to want to sleep there.

HENRY (*crossing to* R *of the sofa*) Did she say so?

CYNTHIA. Not in so many words.

(HENRY *and* CYNTHIA *exchange glances*)

SARAH. That means she knows something.

HENRY. She may not want to sleep there in case it awakens memories of father.

SARAH. Or memories of what's up the chimney.

CYNTHIA. Oh, Sarah, don't!

SARAH. Why don't you just ask her?

HENRY. And what do I say? "Oh, Mother, about that body up the chimney . . ." The shock to her mental equilibrium could be permanent.

CYNTHIA. Oh, Henry, what are we going to do?

SARAH. Move over and make room for Flaherty.

HENRY. We have to find out if she knows it's there, without her thinking that we think she knows it's there, at the same time she mustn't know that we know it's there, in case she doesn't know it's there.

SARAH. That sounds devastatingly simple.

HENRY. It can be done with the correct psychiatric approach.

CYNTHIA. Then for Pete's sake do it. (*She glances at the hall door*) Ssh!

(MRS D'ARCY *enters from the hall*)

(*She crosses to* R) I've made some coffee, Mrs D'Arcy, will you bring it in?

MRS D'ARCY. Oh, Mr Henry, I never told you. Your financy rang up.

HENRY. Oh, hell! I forgot to call her.

MRS D'ARCY. She says would you ring her at her uncle's, and if you've had a lapse of memory, the number's in the book.

HENRY. What time did she ring?

MRS D'ARCY. Soon after you left for the station. She sounded a bit leery.

CYNTHIA. You should have told me.

MRS D'ARCY. You was in the bath. Your mother's had her things sent up to the spare room. Wanted to have a look at what's been done with the study, though. Where's the key?

CYNTHIA. I seem to have mislaid it.

MRS D'ARCY. Right. (*She crosses to the kitchen door and turns*) Mr Henry, what do you know about Helen of Troy?

HENRY. What? Oh. She had a face that launched a thousand ships.

MRS D'ARCY. She sounds more like a dockyard.

(Mrs D'Arcy *exits to the kitchen*)

Henry (*moving to the telephone*) I must telephone Pamela.

(Flaherty *appears outside the garden door, taps on it and comes into the room. He is still in his working clothes*)

Flaherty. Good day to you.

(*There is an angry silence*)

(*He moves to the sideboard*) I'll have a nip if it's all the same to you. (*He pours a drink*) Vat sixty-nine. I'm acquiring a taste for it. Anyone join me? (*He raises his glass*) Good health. (*He drinks then moves affably* c) There's a lot of cases out there—did you see them?

Henry. We did.

Flaherty. If it rains they'll get soaked.

Henry. I hope they get sodden.

Flaherty. Will I bring them in for you?

Henry. If you attempt to bring that junk in here, Flaherty, I shall throw it out—and you, too.

Flaherty. It's the wrong side of the bed you got out of this morning. What's in them? (*He puts his glass on the table behind the sofa*)

Henry (*moving to* r *of Flaherty*) You know damn well what's in them—Dermot Ignatius Eamon McMorragh—you sent them.

Flaherty. I did? Now, hold on, Mr Walling, I've sent nothing . . . (*He breaks off*) Begod! It couldn't be.

(Flaherty *rushes out to the garden*)

Henry (*moving to the garden door and calling*) I'm warning you, Flaherty—if that rubbish comes in here . . .

(Flaherty *enters from the garden, unwrapping a book*)

Flaherty. Rubbish! Them's me *Encyclopaedias*. (*He sits on the sofa*)

(Henry *moves* c)

Cynthia. You've had your *Encyclopaedias* sent here!

Flaherty. Only on appro. They move quick these fellers—I only saw him last night. (*He examines the book*) Oh, Moroccan leather. Put your hand on that, Mr Walling—soft as a kitten.

Henry. Flaherty! I have no wish to stroke your *Encyclopaedia*. Take it outside. I'll give you your cheque and you can go.

Flaherty. Not till I've swept your chimneys. I want to fulfil my obligations or I wouldn't feel like taking your money. (*He turns over the pages of the book*)

Henry. You don't have to take it. Flaherty, I'm speaking to you.

Flaherty. Hey! There's a bit about your sort of thing—psychiatry. Did you know that?

HENRY (*crossing above the sofa to the fireplace*) I should—I wrote it.

FLAHERTY. Did you, now? (*He leans over the back of the sofa and picks up his drink*) That impresses me, Mr Walling. To think of me sitting here drinking your whisky.

HENRY. I do—and I find it most unpleasant.

FLAHERTY (*tapping the book*) There's another bit about philosophy, too, Mr Walling—you never wrote that.

HENRY (*turning on him*) Flaherty!

(MRS D'ARCY *enters from the kitchen carrying a tray with coffee for four*)

CYNTHIA (*indicating the coffee-table*) Put it down here, Mrs D'Arcy.

(MRS D'ARCY *crosses and puts the tray on the coffee-table*)

FLAHERTY. Ah, coffee. If me poor old mother was here, she'd want tea. She used to say, "Tea is better than all your whisky." Did you ever hear such nonsense!

MRS D'ARCY. I didn't know he was here. I'll get another cup. (*She crosses to the kitchen door*)

HENRY. Mr Flaherty won't be having any coffee or tea, thank you, Mrs D'Arcy. He's—going to sweep the chimney.

MRS D'ARCY (*confidentially*) I'll get another cup in case you want to slap him on the couch.

FLAHERTY. That feller never went to work on your nose, then?

MRS D'ARCY. It's going to be Grecian—Helen of Troy.

(MRS D'ARCY *exits to the kitchen.* CYNTHIA *pours the coffee*)

FLAHERTY. What a hope! That face wouldn't launch a canoe. There's a bit in the books about ornithology—she's like one of them tropical birds.

(MRS D'ARCY *re-enters*)

MRS D'ARCY. Who's a tropical bird?

HENRY. That will be all, Mrs D'Arcy.

(MRS D'ARCY *shrugs and exits to the kitchen*)

FLAHERTY. Sure, I didn't realize ye'd made arrangements for me to stay here.

HENRY. We haven't. The sooner you leave the better.

FLAHERTY. I couldn't of stayed, anyway.

(SYBIL *enters from the hall*)

(*He rises and bows*) Good day to you, madam.

SYBIL. Who is this?

HENRY. This is Mr Flaherty.

FLAHERTY. I've come to sweep your chimneys, ma'am. (*He eyes Sybil up and down, then looks thoughtfully above, as though to the chimney on the first floor*) Ah, well!

(Flaherty *shakes his head, moves to the sideboard, sadly puts down his glass and exits to the garden*)

Sybil (*crossing to the sofa*) We had the sweep just before I went away.

Henry. Yes. The truth is, Mr Flaherty isn't really a sweep. He's a patient of mine. (*He crosses to the coffee-table and picks up a cup of coffee*)

Sybil (*sitting on the sofa*) Oh, how sad. Why doesn't he attend your consulting rooms in the usual manner?

Henry (*handing the cup of coffee to Sybil*) I'm humouring him. (*He collects a cup of coffee for himself*) He's harmless, and quite a wealthy man.

Sarah (*rising and crossing to the coffee-table*) Making money hand over fist. (*She takes up a cup of coffee then perches on the table up* r)

Henry. Many wealthy people are a little eccentric. You are yourself in some little ways.

Sybil. Am I? Which ways?

Henry (*crossing above the sofa to* l *of it*) For instance, your reluctance to sleep in father's study. You fight the idea.

Sybil. I wasn't able to put up much of a fight. It was all done while I was in Scotland. By the way, why is it locked, Cynthia?

Cynthia. We locked it to—to keep the dust out, and now I've mislaid the key. (*She rises*) Sugar, Mother?

Sybil. Thank you, dear.

(Cynthia *takes the sugar to Sybil*)

There's another key about somewhere.

Cynthia. Is there? (*She replaces the sugar on the tray*) I wonder if you would excuse us for a minute—(*she moves to Sarah*) I want Sarah to give me a hand with something. (*She pulls Sarah from the table*)

Sarah (*putting her coffee on the table up* r) With what?

Cynthia. Er—in the hall. (*To Sybil*) Those pictures we took from your old bedroom. And I know Henry is anxious to have a talk with mother, aren't you, Henry?

Henry. Oh, yes—yes, I am.

Cynthia. Go along, Sarah.

(Sarah *exits to the hall.*

Cynthia *follows her off.* Henry *takes on his furtive look again as soon as they have gone*)

Sybil. Henry, do stop staring at me like that. You are looking terribly furtive. You haven't been struck off, have you?

Henry (*crossing to* rc) Don't be ridiculous! (*He puts his cup on the coffee table. Suddenly*) Why should I be? What reason have you for saying a thing like that?

Sybil. No reason. Except that you've suddenly started behaving like an expectant father.

HENRY. Mother! (*He moves and sits* R *of Sybil on the sofa*) Mother, there's something I must say to you.

SYBIL. Well, *say* it.

HENRY (*bracing himself*) That sweep I said wasn't a sweep *is* a sweep.

SYBIL (*after a pause*) Say that again, will you, Henry dear.

HENRY. He isn't a wealthy patient at all.

(FLAHERTY *enters from the garden, carrying his brushes*)

He's . . .

FLAHERTY. Where will I begin?

(HENRY *rises*)

SYBIL. There's another room with an open fireplace. It's just across the hall. (*She sips her coffee*)

FLAHERTY (*moving to* R *of Henry; in a whisper*) Get anything from her?

HENRY. No—no. Go and sweep the chimney.

FLAHERTY. Tell her to relax. Will I pull the blinds?

HENRY. No. Leave me alone, will you!

FLAHERTY. You're all tensed up, man. Try her with the shoe.

(FLAHERTY *exits to the hall*)

SYBIL. What was all that hissing about?

HENRY. I was telling you. He's a sweep.

SYBIL. I understood that. What does all this have to do with you looking shifty?

HENRY. I am *not* shifty. I have nothing to be shifty about.

SYBIL. You mean you're looking like that for someone else. Pamela?

HENRY. No. I don't know who makes me look like it. It could be you.

SYBIL. Oh, Henry, don't blame me. I haven't been here for a month.

(MRS D'ARCY *enters from the kitchen. She is holding the black and white shoe*)

MRS D'ARCY. Excuse me. (*She crosses towards the hall door*)

(HENRY *sees the shoe and hurriedly intercepts Mrs D'Arcy*)

HENRY. Where are you going with that? Where did you find it?

MRS D'ARCY. It was under the table when I cleared up this morning. I was just going to ask Miss Cynthia if it's wanted for anything. It's not *yours*, is it, Mr Henry?

HENRY. Mine! Put it down. You—you don't know where it's been.

MRS D'ARCY. I told you. Under the table.

HENRY. Leave it.

(MRS D'ARCY *puts the shoe on the table up* R)

I'll deal with it.

MRS D'ARCY. Right. It's up to you.

(MRS D'ARCY *crosses and exits to the kitchen*)

SYBIL. Take it off the table, Henry. It's unlucky.

(HENRY *picks up the shoe and arranges it significantly on the coffee-table.* SYBIL *eyes it, almost reminiscently*)

HENRY (*sitting on the left arm of the easy chair* RC) Why are you looking at that shoe?

SYBIL. I wondered where it came from.

HENRY. Suppose I said it was up the chimney.

SYBIL. Are you sure you're well, Henry? It's on the table.

HENRY. It's been up the chimney. (*He rises and crosses to Sybil. Desperately*) Flaherty, the sweep, found it. It fell on his head.

SYBIL. It has a nasty sharp point, too. Was he hurt?

HENRY (*moving up* R) No—he wasn't hurt.

(*The telephone rings*)

Oh, blast! Sorry, Mother. (*He crosses to the telephone and lifts the receiver. Into the telephone*) Heath three-o-four-nine . . . Yes, she's here. (*To Sybil*) A personal call for you from Scotland.

(SYBIL *rises, puts her cup on the tray, crosses to Henry and takes the receiver*)

SYBIL. Thank you.

(HENRY *moves up* C)

(*Into the telephone*) Hello . . . Yes, speaking . . . You shouldn't have telephoned. I told you I'd send a wire . . . The train was hours late . . . Oh, fine, dear. Henry met me . . . (*She looks at Henry*) I don't really think he's too well . . . No—I'll call you later on and tell you all about it . . . Well, he's acting in a shifty manner . . .

HENRY. I'm *not* shifty, Mother.

SYBIL (*to Henry*) Shush! (*Into the telephone*) What, dear? . . . No, I'm fine . . . You shouldn't have worried . . . Yes, of course . . . Good-bye. (*She replaces the receiver and turns to Henry*) Bertha McDonald. Nice of her to ring, but she shouldn't fuss.

HENRY. Do you have to tell everyone I'm shifty?

SYBIL (*crossing and sitting on the sofa*) Bertha's my best friend. I tell her everything.

HENRY (*moving to* R *of the sofa*) Mother. About this shoe . . .

SYBIL. Yes, you were telling me. It was up the chimney and fell on Mr Flaherty's head. Not the pointed end, though. What else? But he's only just come to sweep the chimney. (*She rises, moves to*

Henry and pushes him down on to the sofa) Sit down, Henry. I'll get you a drink.

HENRY *(rising; wildly)* I don't *want* a drink. Mr Flaherty swept the chimney yesterday, in father's study.

SYBIL. Go on, dear.

HENRY. Cynthia was going to have a new electric fire fitted for you, so she wanted it swept first.

SYBIL. Well? I think it was very sensible of her.

HENRY *(moving to the coffee-table)* He found this shoe up there. *(He picks up the shoe and waves it at Sybil)*

SYBIL. Don't do that, dear, you might poke it in my eye.

HENRY *(crossing to the fireplace; even more wildly)* There's another one still up there.

SYBIL. He should have got them both down while he was about it.

(HENRY *puts the shoe on the mantelpiece)*

Not that it really matters with the chimney sealed. *(She moves below the sofa)*

HENRY. But that's not all. There was something *else* up there. The person who was *wearing* the shoes.

SYBIL *(sitting on the sofa)* What do you mean?

HENRY. I mean there's a body in the chimney of father's old study. There! I've said it. *(He sits L of Sybil on the sofa)* Now, what do you say to that? Aren't I entitled to look shifty?

SYBIL. A body in our chimney in those shoes?

HENRY. Yes. I've seen it myself. It's been there for years.

SYBIL *(almost to herself)* So *that's* where he put him.

HENRY. Yes, that's where he put him. *What!* What did you say? That's where *who* put *who?*

SYBIL. I thought it was probably the garden. Or the river.

HENRY *(rising and moving above the sofa; beserk)* Mother! Mother! What are you saying? You *knew* there was a body up that chimney?

SYBIL. No, dear. I knew there was a body somewhere—but not up the chimney. What an original idea. *(She rises, crosses to the fireplace and looks at the shoe)*

(HENRY *rushes to the sideboard and pours a drink, his hands shaking)*

HENRY. Oh, lord, this is awful.

(FLAHERTY *enters from the hall and crosses to the garden door)*

FLAHERTY. Just going to take a look at the brush. *(He takes the glass from Henry and drains it)* You're lucky—nobody up that one.

(FLAHERTY *returns the glass to Henry and exits to the garden.* HENRY *pours a fresh drink for himself then goes to* SYBIL *and leads her to the sofa)*

HENRY. Mother, come and sit down.

(SYBIL *sits on the sofa*)

(*He sits* R *of Sybil on the sofa. With forced calm*) Now, listen carefully.

SYBIL. Yes, dear.

HENRY. You knew about this body up the chimney . . .

SYBIL. I've just told you . . .

HENRY. Yes, yes. Do you know who it is?

SYBIL. It'll be Joe Corona.

HENRY. *Who?*

SYBIL. Joe Corona. I didn't really *know* him, but a lot of his friends used to wear that type of shoe. I thought it was familiar.

HENRY. But, Mother! *Who* is he? What is he doing up our chimney?

SYBIL. Your poor father *put* him up there.

HENRY (*rising*) F-f-father?

SYBIL. Yes. He said he was going to hide the body, but he thought it was better that I didn't know where.

HENRY. Ooooh! (*He moves to the sideboard and refills his glass*)

SYBIL. You'll be drunk, Henry.

HENRY. If only I were. If only this was all happening to me in a drunken stupor.

(FLAHERTY *enters from the garden*)

FLAHERTY. It's out. Any luck? (*He takes Henry's drink*)

HENRY (*wildly*) Yes. It's Joe Corona.

(FLAHERTY *drains the glass*)

FLAHERTY. Never heard of him.

(FLAHERTY *hands the glass to Henry and exits to the hall.* HENRY *pours another drink for himself then moves to* R *of the sofa*)

HENRY. Now, Mother dear, let's take this calmly. You say father murdered this man and hid the body?

SYBIL. Oh, no, dear. You see, Joe Corona was a kind of gangster.

HENRY. A—a—gangster?

SYBIL. Yes. Some of your father's clients were very odd people. Night-club owners, that sort of thing. He found them more interesting than what he called three-and-a-half per centers.

HENRY (*shrilly*) But why did he stuff him up a chimney?

SYBIL. Ah, well, that's a long story.

HENRY. We've plenty of time. There's a three-month waiting list at the Old Bailey. (*He sits* R *of Sybil on the sofa*)

SYBIL. I had your grandfather's money so I didn't mind your father working for them. It was more like a hobby for him. You see, your father was so honest.

HENRY. I'm sure he was. No embezzlement or fraud for him—he just stuffed his clients up a flue. What about this Corona?

Sybil. I'm trying to tell you, dear. Your father had a client called Sam Vespata . . .

Henry. Oh, no! Where is he—under the floorboards?

Sybil. No, dear, he's still alive. Sam Vespata was Maltese. He had one of those clubs in Soho. Dealt in the Black Market. He was sent to prison. At his trial he thought your father should have faked some evidence.

Henry Right up father's street.

Sybil. Oh, *no*, dear. He wouldn't do a thing like that. Joe Corona was a—sort of bodyguard for Sam Vespata. After Sam was convicted Corona came here and threatened your father with a gun. There was a struggle. He fell down the stairs and broke his neck.

Henry. Good grief! Where were you?

Sybil. I was evacuated with you children. Your father told me all about it when he came to see us at the week-end.

Henry. Why didn't he call the police?

Sybil. Oh, he didn't want a scandal. And besides, father thought Joe's friends might think he had killed him. Then they would have been after father.

Henry. Oh! I see! But they must have guessed something when Joe didn't come back.

Sybil. A few days later your poor father himself was killed in the air-raid at the *Parisienne*. Oh, dear, I'm so sorry it all had to come out now.

Henry (*rising and crossing to the fireplace*) *You're* sorry! A fine mess he's left for us to clear up. (*He picks up the shoe, looks at it then tosses it into the easy chair down* L. *Desperately*) What can we do?

Sybil. No-one else knows about it, do they? Can't we get rid of the remains?

Henry. Mother! How can you sit there and say that so calmly? (*He crosses above the sofa to* R *of it*) Anyway, the sweep knows. He's already started to blackmail me.

Sybil. Has he? What are you going to do?

Henry. I'm going to buy him an *Encyclopaedia Britannica*—in Moroccan leather.

Sybil. He seems rather an enterprising man. Is he co-operative?

Henry. He should be, in return for an *Encyclopaedia Britannica* at a hundred and eighty guineas. You seem to have no idea of the awful position we're in. Suppose this were to get out? What will Pamela think? (*He moves up* C)

Sybil. Were you thinking of telling her?

Henry. How could I?

Sybil. Then don't. I think I know a simple way out.

Henry. There *is* no simple way out.

Sybil (*rising*) We'll see. (*She crosses to the hall door*) Meanwhile, I shall go upstairs and unpack and have a little rest. When I come down I'd like a word with that sweep.

Henry (*moving to* L *of Sybil*) Now, Mother! Please!

SYBIL. Don't get so *excited*, Henry. Try not to think about it.

(SYBIL *exits to the hall.* HENRY *moves* C.
MRS D'ARCY *enters from the kitchen and crosses to the coffee-table*)

MRS D'ARCY (*picking up the coffee-tray*) How did you get on with the sweep? Is he violent?

HENRY. Eh?

MRS D'ARCY. Call for me if you want any help. I used to be a nurse in the war. That's where I met D'Arcy. Poor feller, he'd sat on an incendiary bomb. Lying flat on his face in bed. That's how it was we got married. He took a fancy to me before he ever saw me. He was as good as his word, bless him, though, when he eventually turned over. (*She crosses to the kitchen door and turns*) Did you ring your fiancy up?

HENRY. No—no. I'd better do it now.

(MRS D'ARCY *exits to the kitchen.* HENRY *goes to the telephone and lifts the receiver, but he has not the courage to dial and replaces it*)

(*He moves* RC *and speaks as though on the telephone*) Hello, Pam. Sorry I couldn't come. Mother says the body up the chimney is Joe Corona. (*He shakes his head*) Pamela——

(CYNTHIA *and* SARAH *enters from the hall, look at Henry and exchange glances*)

—my dear, I'm sorry I can't come but mother says father stuffed . . .

CYNTHIA. What on earth is the matter with you?

HENRY. I'm just trying to imagine what I shall say to Pamela.

SARAH (*crossing to* R *of Henry*) Any luck with mother?

HENRY. Any luck! Oh, yes. He's Joe Corona.

SARAH. Joe Corona?

HENRY. Mother says father stuffed him up there.

CYNTHIA (*moving to* R *of Sarah*) *Father* did?

HENRY. Yes. It was practically his last act before he died. He got himself bombed and left his children a legacy of a dead gangster in the study chimney. (*He moves up* L)

SARAH (*crossing to* C) You mean to say mother knew about it all the time?

HENRY (*wildly*) She didn't know where it was; she just knew it was about the place somewhere. (*He moves and sits on the right arm of the sofa*) She probably thought Mrs D'Arcy would come across Joe one day and pop him in the dustbin.

CYNTHIA (*moving to* R *of Henry*) Henry, this is terrible! (*Desperately*) Our own father—a murderer.

HENRY. He didn't murder him. He threw him downstairs.

SARAH. That makes all the difference.

HENRY. No, no, it was an accident.

SARAH. Oh, that's not so bad, then.

CYNTHIA (*crossing above the sofa to the fireplace*) To think mother has known all these years.

SARAH (*crossing and sitting on the left arm of the easy chair* RC) You know mother. If she can't see it—it's not there.

CYNTHIA. How on earth did father ever get mixed up with a lot of gangsters—a respectable solicitor?

HENRY. He wasn't respectable. According to mother he dealt with some of the shadiest characters in London.

CYNTHIA (*sitting on the sofa*) But what did she say, exactly? I can't imagine even mother shrugging the whole thing off—now it's been discovered.

HENRY. Can't you? You tackle her when she comes down. She thinks she has a simple way out. She told me not to worry. Did you ever hear such drivel?

(FLAHERTY *enters from the hall*)

FLAHERTY (*crossing to the sideboard*) Just a small one. (*He pours a drink*) Your little rule about not drinkin' in the mornings has gone all to hell.

SARAH. Does Mr Flaherty know who it is?

FLAHERTY (*moving* C) Feller named Corona, Mr Walling is after tellin' me. (*He drinks*)

HENRY (*rising and moving to* L *of Flaherty*) My mother says she wants to speak to you, Mr Flaherty. She's a little unbalanced, you know. If she has any hare-brained schemes you must ignore them.

FLAHERTY. Was this Corona feller a friend of hers? Is she after puttin' him up there herself?

HENRY. Don't you dare suggest such a thing about my mother.

FLAHERTY. Beggin' your pardon. Who put him up there, then?

HENRY. My father.

FLAHERTY. Ah, well, that's different.

HENRY. You don't understand. This Corona was a gangster. He came to murder my father.

FLAHERTY. I'm no lover of the police—but they can be helpful in cases of that sort.

HENRY. He couldn't call the police. He had very good reasons.

FLAHERTY (*knowingly*) I understand.

(SYBIL *enters from the hall*)

SYBIL. Finished that room, Mr Flaherty?

FLAHERTY. More or less, ma'am.

SYBIL (*crossing to* R *of the sofa*) Good. I want to have a little talk with you. Have you found the key to the study yet, Cynthia?

CYNTHIA (*rising and moving* L) No—er . . .

HENRY. I have it.

SYBIL. Give it to me, then.

HENRY. What do you want it for?

SYBIL (*firmly*) Give it to me, please.

HENRY (*taking out the key*) Now, Mother, I insist on that room staying closed.

SYBIL. It will stay closed.

(SARAH *rises*)

(*She moves and takes the key from Henry*) Now, if you'll excuse me, I want to speak to Mr Flaherty alone. (*She sits on the sofa*)

CYNTHIA (*moving to Sybil*) Mother—Henry has told us everything and . . .

SYBIL. Henry doesn't know what to do. I do.

HENRY (*moving to the kitchen door*) Come along, Cynthia—Sarah. Remember what I said, Flaherty. (*He looks warningly at Sybil*)

FLAHERTY. Ah, sure. Don't be worryin', Mr Walling. I'm used to managing such people. Me cousin Seamus spent three years in the County Asylum. He used to walk about on stilts and say he was Brian Boru.

(HENRY *gives a despairing look at Sarah and Cynthia and exits to the kitchen.*
SARAH *and* CYNTHIA *follow him off*)

SYBIL. Will you have another drink, Mr Flaherty?

FLAHERTY. That's kind of you. (*He moves to the sideboard and refills his glass*) Will you join me?

SYBIL. No, thank you.

FLAHERTY (*moving* C) He's a grand feller, your son. Writing bits for *Encyclopaedias* and all.

SYBIL. He's very clever, but like all psychiatrists he thinks everyone is slightly mad. I suppose he has to. It's to his advantage.

FLAHERTY. Yis. In the same way as I like to see a chimney afire.

SYBIL. Exactly. I expect he told you I was unbalanced, didn't he?

FLAHERTY (*uncomfortably*) I wouldn't say that.

SYBIL. No, you wouldn't say it, but he did. So, you found Joe Corona up the chimney, then?

FLAHERTY. I did. One of his shoes cracked me on the head.

SYBIL. And you decided to blackmail my son.

FLAHERTY. Well—(*he pauses*) he said he'd make it worth me while, you see . . .

SYBIL. If I know my son he'd think ten shillings would make it worth your while. But you decided you'd like an *Encyclopaedia*.

FLAHERTY. It was a good opportunity. I've them outside—I'll bring them in.

SYBIL. I'll see them later. Are you satisfied with an *Encyclopaedia?*

FLAHERTY. Satisfied?

SYBIL. It doesn't seem a great deal to ask for. You should have demanded more. My son is very well off, you know. He only attends rich lunatics.

FLAHERTY (*thoughtfully*) Maybe I could have fixed up a little pension.

SYBIL. An excellent idea. And what about me? I'm quite wealthy, you know.

FLAHERTY. Well, it did cross my mind.

SYBIL. Good. I shouldn't like to think you were a man who missed his opportunities. The *Encyclopaedia* was really just a start.

FLAHERTY. It was. I thought it over and decided that asking for a few books sort of puts the affair more on a social scale. Blackmail a feller for the price of a dinner and he'll enjoy eating with you, but bite the same feller's ear for ten shillings and he'll throw you in the bog.

SYBIL. Had you made up your mind what you were going to ask me for? I presume you wouldn't just "bite my ear" as you put it, for cash.

FLAHERTY. Well, no—no, I hadn't made up me mind. (*He moves down* L, *puts his glass on the mantelpiece and picks up the shoe from the easy chair down* L) It occurred to me that ye might like to help me buy a house—as a sort of investment, you understand.

SYBIL. I do. What is your house worth?

FLAHERTY. I think I'd get it for two thousand, five hundred. But I'd like to spend a bit on repairs. The landlord is a terrible feller, can't get so much as a dustbin lid out of him.

SYBIL. Let's call it square at three thousand, shall we?

FLAHERTY (*gulping*) Now, wait—(*he moves to* L *of Sybil*) are ye *offerin'* me three thousand pounds?

SYBIL. Sit down, Mr Flaherty. I have a little proposition to put to you.

(FLAHERTY *sits* L *of Sybil on the sofa, still clutching the shoe*)

I gather there isn't very much left of Mr Corona up the chimney?

FLAHERTY. Not that I can see. He's wrapped up, you know.

SYBIL. He would be. My husband was very tidy. Now, for three thousand pounds would you be prepared to take him away and bury him decently?

FLAHERTY. Take him away—how would I do that?

SYBIL. It's very simple. When a sweep leaves a house he generally has one or two bags with him. Soot and so on. I don't think you'd find any difficulty.

FLAHERTY. Three thousand, you say?

SYBIL. Yes. I can have it in the morning. I don't think you need have any scruples about where you bury Joe, he was only a murdering thug.

FLAHERTY. I wasn't thinkin' of taking him into church for a funeral service. (*He rises*) I'll take a look up there now.

SYBIL (*holding out the key*) Mr Flaherty, you'll need the key.

FLAHERTY (*taking the key and crossing to* C) Would I do it now? In broad daylight?

Sybil. If anyone saw a sweep in the middle of the night carrying a sack that *would* be suspicious.

Flaherty. Right you are. Mrs Walling, if it's unbalanced you are—may I always do me business with crackpots. (*He puts the shoe on the table up* RC *then goes to the sideboard and pours a drink*)

Sybil (*rising and moving to* L *of Flaherty*) Now, we shan't say anything about this to my son or the girls until you've gone. I'll go and keep them occupied while you go and collect Joe.

Flaherty. Begob, it's a pity you weren't in the old country when the Black and Tans was with us. Lloyd George would have sued for peace in a week. (*He raises his glass*) Here's to you. (*He drinks*)

(Sybil *moves to the kitchen door*)

There's just one thing.

Sybil (*stopping and turning*) What's that?

Flaherty. Tell you what. Make it four thousand.

Sybil. Mr Flaherty, now you're being greedy. My husband was a solicitor, you know, and there is such a thing as being an accessory after the act.

Flaherty. Hold on a minute. Are you trying to blackmail me? (*He pauses*) There wouldn't be any doubt I'd get me money?

Sybil. No more doubt than that you wouldn't come back and raise the price—I'm prepared to trust you.

Flaherty (*moving to Sybil*) It's a deal. (*He shakes hands with Sybil*) There's no objection to me still havin' the *Encyclopaedia?*

Sybil. Not at all. My son can well afford it. Give me five minutes or so.

Flaherty. I will.

(Sybil *exits to the kitchen.* Flaherty *wanders to the table, picks up the shoe and examines it.*

Rosita Hernandez *enters from the garden. She is an attractive, Spanish-looking girl in her teens. She is holding a parcel.* Flaherty *drops the shoe and looks at her*)

Rosita. Hello. Is this Dr Walling's house?

Flaherty. It is.

(Rosita *sweeps to the sofa and flings herself down, prostrate, clutching her parcel. She lies back, her head* L, *and puts her feet up*)

(*He moves to* R *of the sofa*) Hey, what are ye at? Ye can't sleep there.

Rosita. Fetch Dr Walling.

Flaherty (*taken aback*) Is it one of his patients ye are?

Rosita. Yes, he's my father.

Flaherty. He's *what?* Now, look here, he's not married at all.

Rosita (*sitting up*) Fetch him! I've developed a new symptom. (*She waves the parcel*)

Flaherty. I'm a little busy right now. I've a job to do. His sister will be in any minute.

ROSITA (*swinging her feet to the floor*) *No!* They mustn't see me. I must see Dr Walling alone. He understands me. (*She lies back*) Tell him I'm unbalanced again.

FLAHERTY. You look all right to me.

ROSITA (*sitting up*) Oh, no! (*She pulls Flaherty on to the sofa*) Do you want to hear about my unhappy childhood? My stepfather trod on my pet snake and threw D.D.T. on my scorpion.

FLAHERTY (*uneasily*) Did he now? He sounds an awkward sort of feller.

ROSITA. You wouldn't do that to your daughter, would you?

FLAHERTY. Not at all. Nothing I like better than snakes an' scorpions about the place.

ROSITA. Until I met Dr Walling I was unwanted.

FLAHERTY. You don't tell me!

ROSITA. He is always so calm, so gentle.

FLAHERTY. Is he now!

ROSITA (*indignantly*) He won't see me any more because he thinks I'm cured—but I can prove I'm not. (*She displays the parcel*) If only I could see him alone—I could tell him everything.

FLAHERTY (*looking at the key*) I think I know the very place. (*He rises, pulls Rosita to her feet and leads her* R) Come with me.

ROSITA (*stopping*) Can I trust you?

FLAHERTY. You'll have to if you want to see Dr Walling.

(*There is a knock at the front door*)

Come on, now. While there's still room in the house.

(FLAHERTY *and* ROSITA *exit quickly to the hall.*

MRS D'ARCY *enters from the kitchen and looks at herself in the mirror. There is another knock at the front door.*

MRS D'ARCY *crosses and exits to the hall*)

MRS D'ARCY (*off*) Good afternoon, sir.

HARDY (*off*) Inspector Hardy, Scotland Yard.

MRS D'ARCY (*off*) Oh. You'd better come in.

(MRS D'ARCY *enters from the hall.*

INSPECTOR HARDY *and* SERGEANT BRAY *follow her on.* BRAY *is fascinated by Mrs D'Arcy's nose.*

HENRY *and* CYNTHIA *enter from the kitchen.* CYNTHIA *moves to the fireplace.* HARDY *crosses to* C. BRAY *stands* RC. MRS D'ARCY *is* R)

HENRY (*as he enters*) Who was that, Mrs D'Arcy? (*He sees Hardy*) Oh.

MRS D'ARCY. It's the police. Scotland Yard.

HENRY (*crossing to* C) Oh, yes. (*He stops dead*) *Scotland Yard!*

HARDY. Good morning—I'm Inspector Hardy.

HENRY. How do you do?

HARDY. And this is Sergeant Bray.

HENRY. Y-yes.

HARDY. We're from the Missing Persons Bureau.

HENRY (*moving to the sideboard*) The Missing Persons Bureau. (*He pours a drink for himself*) H-have a whisky, Inspector?

HARDY. No, thank you, sir. (*He picks up the shoe from the table*) You'll have bad luck, sir.

HENRY. What? That's mine.

HARDY. Is it now? (*He looks at Henry's feet*) I'd have said you took a smaller size.

HENRY. I—I do. But I have bunions. And when they hurt me badly I wear those shoes.

HARDY. Good idea. (*He moves down* C *and shows the shoe to Bray*) Sergeant Bray here has bunions.

HENRY. Oh, really! I'd give them to him—but I've only got the one.

HARDY. *One?*

HENRY. One pair, that is.

HARDY. I don't think he would want them—they're hardly regulation style, eh, Sergeant?

BRAY (*looking at Mrs D'Arcy*) Eh? Oh, no, sir.

MRS D'ARCY. Could I go, sir, please, if the sergeant's quite finished with my nose?

HENRY. Yes—yes, Mrs D'Arcy.

(MRS D'ARCY *gives Bray a look and exits to the hall.* HARDY *puts the shoe under the table up* R)

CYNTHIA. Sit down, Inspector, won't you?

HARDY (*sitting on the sofa*) Thank you, madam. Now, Dr Walling, I'm afraid we've left this rather late in the day.

HENRY. Yes, you have—that is to say, what's rather late in the day?

HARDY. We should have come about it before.

HENRY. Oh? Should you?

HARDY. Yes. You do know, of course, she's missing?

HENRY. She?

HARDY. Yes—Rosita Hernandez.

HENRY (*with elation*) Rosita! (*He moves to the easy chair* RC *and sits*) Oh, yes, I knew *she* was missing. Very sad—very sad indeed.

HARDY. When did you last see her?

HENRY. Not since last week when her stepfather brought her to see me at Welbeck Street. You have no idea where she is, then?

HARDY. No, sir. Her stepfather, the ambassador, is naturally very anxious, and as he's a member of the Diplomatic Corps, we have to be on our toes. Senor Hernandez seems to think she might try to contact you.

HENRY. Well, if she does I'll let you know.

HARDY. I'm sure you will, sir. But I'm afraid it's not quite as simple as that. You see, the girl has stolen something.

HENRY. Stolen something? I never suspected kleptomania.

HARDY. Well, sir, apparently she went to Asprey's of Bond Street and asked to see a silver loving cup, then calmly walked out and went down into the Underground with it.

HENRY. I see.

HARDY. Of course, we know the girl isn't a criminal, but she must be found, the Home Secretary is on our tails. I gather the Foreign Secretary is on *his* tail.

HENRY. Very awkward. If she turns up I'll let you know at once. (*He rises*)

HARDY (*rising*) Thank you, sir. It's rather a tricky case.

HENRY. Don't worry. I can cope with her—I understand her condition.

(SYBIL *and* SARAH *enter from the kitchen.* SARAH *stands with Cynthia at the fireplace*)

SYBIL (*crossing to* C) Oh, visitors, Henry?

HENRY. Yes, Mother. These gentlemen are from Scotland Yard.

SYBIL. Oh, dear! (*She moves to the sofa and sits*)

HENRY (*quickly*) They're trying to trace one of my patients who's run away. They're just leaving.

HARDY. Dr Walling, I suppose there is no possibility of the girl being here without you knowing?

HENRY. What do you mean?

HARDY. It might save time if we had a look around. (*He crosses to the hall door*)

SYBIL. No. There's nobody here.

HARDY. You wouldn't know if she were, Mrs Walling. She may have hidden the silver cup somewhere.

CYNTHIA (*crossing to* C) C-couldn't you leave it for a day or so, Inspector? We—we've just had the place decorated.

HENRY. We're in a muddle.

SARAH (*moving to* L *of the sofa*) Yes. The rooms are in a shocking state.

HARDY. Don't worry, ladies. We shan't be making any formal report on the general tidiness of the place. Perhaps one of you would like to come round with us. Then you can rush in the rooms and make the beds before we go in, eh, Sergeant?

(HARDY *gives a laugh which is shared by* BRAY *but no-one else*)

Now, where shall we start?

CYNTHIA. I'll show you round, Inspector. (*She crosses to the hall door*)

HENRY. Oh, Cynthia, there's one room the Inspector won't have to look in. It's locked. Inspector, my father's old study has been locked for years.

SYBIL (*rising*) No! No, they mustn't go there.

HENRY (*leading Hardy up* LC) Excuse my mother. You can see why we keep it locked. She can't bear the thought of anyone entering father's old study.

HARDY. We'll leave that, then. If there's no other means of entry.

HENRY. Oh, no—it's on the first floor. The window is locked, too.

SYBIL (*faintly*) Henry . . .

(FLAHERTY *enters from the hall. He carries a full sack on his shoulder*)

HARDY. Who is this?

HENRY. This is Mr Flaherty—the sweep. These gentlemen are from Scotland Yard.

HARDY. What's in that sack?

FLAHERTY. Ah sure, it's soot, Officer—out o' the chimney.

HARDY. If the girl has been here she might have had a chance to slip the silver cup inside. Put it in the garden, Flaherty.

(FLAHERTY *crosses to the garden door*)

(*To Bray*) Take a look in it right away, Sergeant.

BRAY *crosses towards the garden door*. SYBIL *gives a wail and faints as* BRAY *passes her. He stops to catch Sybil as—*

the CURTAIN *falls*

ACT III

SCENE—*The same. Immediately following.*

When the CURTAIN *rises, everyone is in the same positions as they were at the end of the previous Act.* BRAY *is supporting the fainting* SYBIL C. HENRY *and* HARDY *are up* LC. FLAHERTY *is at the garden door.* CYNTHIA *is* R *and* SARAH *is* L.

SARAH. Mother!

(CYNTHIA *and* SARAH *rush to Sybil. They take* SYBIL *from Bray and sit her in the easy chair* RC. CYNTHIA *kneels* R *of Sybil,* SARAH *kneels* L *of her*)

HENRY. What on earth is the matter with her? (*He moves to* L *of Sybil*) Mother!

HARDY. I'm sorry about this, Mr Walling.

HENRY. It's not your fault, Inspector. All the excitement, the—er—police and so on, has been too much for her. My mother is sometimes—shall we say, emotionally unbalanced.

HARDY (*moving down* L *of the sofa and nodding knowingly*) I understand.

CYNTHIA (*rising*) She's only fainted. I'll make her a cup of tea. (*She crosses to the kitchen door*) Stay with her, Sarah.

(CYNTHIA *exits to the kitchen*)

HENRY (*moving to Flaherty*) I think you had better collect the rest of your equipment and go, Flaherty.

FLAHERTY. Mr Walling . . .

HARDY. Leave that sack. You can collect it later.

(FLAHERTY *puts his sack, out of sight, outside the garden door*)

HENRY (*moving to Sybil*) Now, Sarah, don't fuss. Mother will be all right. (*He takes Sybil's pulse*)

FLAHERTY. Mr Walling, I'm not quite finished. There's another little job to be done.

HENRY. Then do it and go.

FLAHERTY. The chance u'd be a fine thing.

(FLAHERTY *looks in the direction of the sack then crosses and exits to the hall*)

SARAH (*rising and moving to the kitchen door*) Perhaps you would like to start with the kitchen, Inspector.

(BRAY *moves to the garden door and touches the sack*)

HARDY. We might as well. (*To Bray*) Better leave that for the moment, Sergeant. You'll get black.

(BRAY *moves above the sofa. His hands are black and he looks a little disgruntled.* SYBIL *comes round. She sees Bray's hands*)

SYBIL. Oh! The body! What did you tell them, Henry?
HENRY (*muttering*) Shut *up*, Mother! (*Louder*) Don't talk, dear.
HARDY. What's this?
SYBIL. You mustn't hold the children responsible. Their father hid the body.

(HARDY *crosses down* R)

HENRY. Mother! Please be quiet. Don't take any notice of her ramblings, Inspector. (*He looks meaningly at Hardy*) She isn't well.
SARAH (*moving and kneeling* L *of Sybil*) Mother, you mustn't talk any more. You must rest.
SYBIL. No, Sarah. I think it's best to lay our cards on the table. I think that . . .
HENRY (*interrupting*) Attacks like this after a faint are quite frequent.
SYBIL. Don't dither, Henry. We've nothing to hide. Don't worry about the body. I'm sure the Inspector will see we get no unpleasant publicity if we give him a full explanation.

(HARDY, *who has looked a little lost, recovers*)

HARDY. Leave it to us, Mrs Walling. There won't be any publicity.

(BRAY *moves to* L *of the sofa*)

SYBIL. You mean you really can hush it up?
HARDY. I see no reason why we should say anything. Do you, Sergeant?
BRAY. No, sir. Just not write it in my book.

(HENRY *crosses down* L)

HARDY. There! That's all settled, Mrs Walling.
SYBIL. Thank you very much, Inspector. That's very kind of you. To think we've had all this worry for nothing, Henry. You've really no need to give Mr Flaherty the *Encyclopaedia*—although perhaps there is a moral obligation. After all, he did find the body—*and* didn't tell the police.
SARAH. Mother! Stop *talking*.
HENRY. I'm sorry, Inspector . . .
SYBIL. I don't want Mr Flaherty to get into any trouble.
HARDY. He won't, I promise you that. (*He gives a meaning glance at Henry, then moves to the kitchen door*)

(SARAH *rises and moves up* RC)

I may as well see the kitchen now, sir. No need for you to come, Miss Walling. The housekeeper can show me round. Better stay with your mother. Forget about that body, Mrs Walling. All in a day's work for us. Come along, Sergeant.

(HARDY *and* BRAY *exit to the kitchen. As soon as they have gone* HENRY *dives for the sideboard and pours a drink for himself*)

SARAH (*moving to the sofa and collapsing on it*) That was a close one.

SYBIL. Yes. I had a feeling things would go right.

HENRY (*spluttering out his drink*) Go right! What's the matter with you? You *told* him about the body! (*He moves up* R) If he'd believed you we'd all be on the way to—to Pentonville. (*He moves to* R *of Sybil*)

SYBIL. But he found it.

HENRY. Didn't you hear him? He hasn't even *looked* upstairs yet.

SYBIL. But Flaherty's sack. It's out there. The sergeant found it there—he was about to examine it when I fainted.

SARAH. No, he caught you when you fainted.

HENRY (*impatiently*) What has a bag of soot to do with it, anyway? He's only looking for a silver cup. The body is up the chimney, in case you've forgotten.

SYBIL. No, it isn't.

SARAH. What do you mean?

SYBIL. I paid Flaherty to bring it down in his sack.

HENRY. You—you mean Joe Corona is in that sack out there?

SYBIL. Yes. I thought it such a simple way to solve the whole thing.

HENRY. Oh, *no!* (*He rushes to the garden door*)

(SARAH *rises and rushes to the garden door*)

Look out! There's the sergeant. (*He moves from the garden door to the table up* R)

SARAH (*moving above the easy chair* RC) But, Mummy, why did you ask Flaherty to do it?

SYBIL. I told you. It settled everything. He offered to bury Joe in some discreet spot and . . . (*She breaks off*) You say the sergeant *hasn't* looked in the sack?

HENRY (*dazed*) No. Not yet.

SYBIL. Then he doesn't know there is a body. We must get rid of it before he does.

(SARAH *moves to the window*)

SARAH. The sergeant is in the garden. He'd see us—the beast. (*She waves cheerily to Bray*) Hello.

HENRY. I'll get Flaherty. (*He moves to the hall door*) He's being paid to do it—I presume you did pay him?

SYBIL. Yes, I'm going to help him buy his house. He only needs three thousand pounds.

Henry. Three thousand pounds!

Sybil. I can't understand why the inspector was so casual about it.

Henry. Because he thinks you're a raving lunatic. (*He looks at Sybil*) I'm not sure he isn't right. (*He moves up* R)

(Sarah *moves to the sideboard.*
Cynthia *enters from the kitchen, carrying a tray of tea for one*)

Cynthia (*crossing and putting the tray on the coffee-table*) How are you, Mother? (*She moves the table nearer to Sybil*)

Sybil. Better, thank you, dear. (*She pours a cup of tea for herself*) I can manage.

Cynthia. I'll have to stay with them. Mrs D'Arcy isn't very co-operative.

Henry. So much the better. (*He moves to the garden door*) You stay here. (*He calls to Bray*) Lovely day . . . Yes, beautiful. (*He turns*) He's still there. The damned snooper.

Cynthia. Who is, Henry?

Henry. The sergeant. (*He moves* C)

Cynthia. What is the matter with you, Henry? The inspector won't look in father's old study now we've explained that it's always kept locked. They're quite satisfied.

Henry. It so happens that Joe Corona isn't there any more.

Cynthia. Not *there?*

Henry. No. He's in the garden.

Cynthia. What!

Henry. In Flaherty's sack—by the dahlias.

Cynthia. H-how did he get there?

Henry. Mother had a brilliant idea. She paid Flaherty some fantastic sum to inter him discreetly. Now he's waiting out there in a sack for collection by Sergeant Bray. (*He crosses down* R)

Sybil. Why can't we explain it all to the inspector? He seems a very pleasant man.

Henry. He'd damned soon cease to be pleasant if he knew there was a body in that sack, take my word for it.

(Mrs D'Arcy *enters from the kitchen*)

Mrs D'Arcy (*crossing to* C; *aggressively*) I think I'm entitled to an explanation.

Cynthia. Mrs D'Arcy, please. My mother isn't well.

Mrs D'Arcy. I'm sorry about that, but I've never had no trouble with the police before and I don't intend to start now.

Sybil. Whatever's the matter?

Mrs D'Arcy. That inspector, he's going through my kitchen as though I was Jack the Ripper.

Henry. He's searching for someone.

Mrs D'Arcy. Who?

HENRY. A patient of mine. A girl who ran away from home—he thinks she may be hiding here.

MRS D'ARCY. He's searching my bread-bin. What is she—a midget?

CYNTHIA. She has stolen something and may have hidden it.

MRS D'ARCY. What?

SARAH. A loving cup.

MRS D'ARCY. That'll be the day when someone hides a loving cup in my bread-bin. What with that sweep round the bend and now this girl, I might as well be working in Colney Hatch.

(CYNTHIA *crosses to the fireplace*)

HENRY. Don't worry, Mrs D'Arcy. The girl isn't here, the search is just a formality.

MRS D'ARCY. From the way that sergeant looks at me, you'd think she was hiding in my nose.

(HARDY *enters from the kitchen*)

HARDY. All clear out there.

MRS D'ARCY (*crossing to the kitchen door*) I just hope you've left everything tidy.

HARDY. As tidy as it was when I came.

MRS D'ARCY. I'll let you know if I find any loving cups or nut-cases in the fridge.

HARDY. I've looked in the fridge.

MRS D'ARCY. You've got a cheek.

(MRS D'ARCY *snorts and exits to the kitchen*)

CYNTHIA (*crossing to the hall door*) Can I show you upstairs, Inspector?

HARDY. Please.

SARAH (*moving up* C; *eagerly*) You'll need some help. I'll get the sergeant.

HARDY. Don't bother, miss. I can manage on my own. I don't expect for a moment that Miss Hernandez is here. However . . .

(SARAH *moves and sits on the sofa*)

HENRY (*moving to the garden door*) It's as well to be sure. I'll call the sergeant.

HARDY. No. Let him finish what he's doing, sir.

(FLAHERTY *enters from the hall, carrying some of his brushes*)

(*He moves to* L *of Sybil*) Feeling better, Mrs Walling?

HENRY (*moving down* C) She's much better, but you mustn't excite her.

HARDY. I won't. Don't worry any more. We'll dispose of the body.

(FLAHERTY *stares goggle-eyed at Hardy*)

Sybil. V-very kind of you, Inspector.

Hardy. Happy to be of service, madam. (*He crosses to* L *of Flaherty*) Ah, Flaherty, found any more bodies?

Flaherty. Have I *what?*

Hardy. Mrs Walling tells me you found a body. (*He nods briefly in Sybil's direction*)

Flaherty. She—she does? Now, look here, Inspector, this is all their idea . . .

Hardy (*interrupting*) That's all right, man. I understand. (*He winks*) Must have been disconcerting for you. Was it up the chimney?

Flaherty. Sure, it was. *Eh?*

Hardy. Must have been a big surprise for you.

Flaherty. It was and all. One of its shoes cracked me on the head.

Hardy. Very dangerous. (*He smiles*) Better take care in the future. Wear a crash helmet or something.

Flaherty (*staring at him*) Aye—I'll do that.

Hardy (*enjoying himself*) Where is he? It was a man, I suppose.

Flaherty. Oh, sure. It was Joe Corona.

(Sarah *rises*)

Hardy. Joe Corona—the name sounds familiar.

Sarah. Cigars, Inspector.

Hardy. Well, leave it to us. I've told Mrs Walling we'll dispose of the body. By the way, where have you put him?

Flaherty. In me sack.

Hardy. Best place. (*To Sybil*) Very convenient for us to deal with.

Henry (*looking out of the garden door*) He's looking in it!

(Sarah *runs to* L *of the garden door.* Flaherty *and* Cynthia *move up* C)

Sybil (*rising and moving up* C) No! He mustn't!

(Bray *enters from the garden. The others back away from him. His hands are very black and so is his face*)

Hardy (*pushing through the others to Bray*) Anything in there, Sergeant?

(Sarah *and* Flaherty *are above the sofa.* Sybil *is up* LC. Henry *and* Cynthia *move* R)

Bray. Yes, sir.

Hardy. What?

Bray. Soot.

Sybil. But—but the body. Joe Corona.

Hardy. You didn't come across a body in there by any chance, Sergeant?

Bray. Not that I noticed. sir.

HARDY. Must be in one of your other sacks, eh, Flaherty?

FLAHERTY (*shaken*) Yis. You've hit the nail on the head, Inspector.

(SARAH *moves to the fireplace*)

HARDY. Fine. Give it to us when we go.

FLAHERTY. Yes, sir.

HARDY. Right. Now, Miss Walling, I'll take a quick look round the rest of the house.

CYNTHIA (*crossing to the hall door*) Come along. We'll look across the hall downstairs first. Although I think it's all a waste of time.

HARDY (*crossing to Cynthia*) Fine. I'm sure you're right.

(MRS D'ARCY *enters from the kitchen.* SYBIL *moves to the sideboard*)

MRS D'ARCY. That sergeant is rushin' in and out of the bushes like a Boy Scout. (*She looks at Bray*) Good grief! I thought you was one of the Black and White Minstrels.

BRAY (*eyeing her nose*) Could I wash before I look upstairs, sir?

MRS D'ARCY. You'd better. I don't want nobody round my beds in that state. Go on, the sink will do.

(MRS D'ARCY *exits to the kitchen.*
BRAY *follows her off.*
HARDY *and* CYNTHIA *exit to the hall*)

FLAHERTY. Now, what the hell is going on here? What sort of an inspector is that? Laughing and winking about the body.

HENRY. He thinks the body is an hallucination of my mother's.

SYBIL. Where *is* it, Mr Flaherty? I thought he was in the bag of soot. What have you *done* with Joe?

FLAHERTY. He's above. In me other sack. I was just bringin' him down when I seen you and the girl here, so I had to nip back in the room and leave it there.

SARAH (*sitting on the sofa*) Just as well. The inspector won't look there. You locked the door, of course.

FLAHERTY. In a manner of speaking, yes.

HENRY. What does that mean? Have you locked it or haven't you?

FLAHERTY (*sitting on the left arm of the easy chair* RC) It'll be locked right enough.

HENRY. You'd better give me the key, Flaherty, before my mother has any more hare-brained schemes.

FLAHERTY. 'Tis in the room.

HENRY. How can it be if you locked the door—you aren't Houdini.

FLAHERTY. I had to ask the young girl to lock the door. I left her in there.

HENRY. Then knock on the door and ask her for it. (*He does a "take"*) *What* young girl?

FLAHERTY. Rosita, her name is.

HENRY. You've locked Rosita in that room?

SYBIL. With Joe Corona!

FLAHERTY. He'll not bother her.

HENRY (*moving to the sideboard*) Good Lord! She's been here all the time?

SARAH. Surely, Henry, the best thing would be to go and let Rosita out. Then the inspector will take her and he won't look inside the room at all. (*She rises*)

HENRY. Good idea!

SYBIL (*moving* C) We must be careful. Because if the inspector does look in there he might see the other sack—the one with Joe in.

HENRY. We must get Rosita out—suppose *she* looks in the sack.

FLAHERTY. Then the inspector will know she's here right enough. They'll hear her yell at Scotland Yard.

(*There is a knock at the front door*)

HENRY. Who the hell's that? (*He moves to the door* R) See who that is, Sarah—and get rid of them.

(SARAH *crosses and exits to the hall*)

SYBIL. I'll go into the kitchen and keep the sergeant occupied. We don't want him about while you're getting Rosita out.

(SYBIL *exits to the kitchen*)

HENRY. I'd better make sure the inspector isn't on the top floor before we do anything.

FLAHERTY (*rising*) What will I do?

HENRY. Stay here—and as soon as I've let Rosita out—and the police are gone—get that sack out of the house—if you want to see your money.

FLAHERTY. And the *Encyclopaedia*.

(ROSITA *creeps in from the hall.* HENRY *turns to go and nearly bumps into her*)

ROSITA. I am tired of waiting in . . . Dr Walling!

HENRY. Rosita! What are you doing down here?

ROSITA (*taking Henry's hand and drawing him* C) I must speak to you. (*She flings herself on the sofa*)

FLAHERTY. It's a very tired girl she is.

HENRY. Get up. The police are here, you've stolen a cup.

ROSITA. It was a compulsion.

HENRY. A what?

ROSITA. I had a repression. It relieved me. Dr Walling, I've thought of something else from my childhood. You know my stepfather has a big moustache . . .

HENRY. Damn his moustache! What have you done with that cup?

ROSITA. It's upstairs.

HENRY. Go with Mr Flaherty and find it. We must get her out of here. Rosita. You *must* go with Mr Flaherty now. We'll go into your childhood later.

ROSITA. You will examine me, Dr Walling?

HENRY. With a microscope. I'll find you a father, too. (*He takes Rosita's hand and looks at her*)

(THE HONOURABLE PAMELA COLEFAX *enters from the hall. She is in her late twenties, tall and athletic*)

PAMELA (*staring at Henry*) Well! Henry!

HENRY. Pamela. Oh, *hell!* I mean—hello, Pamela darling. How nice of you to come.

PAMELA (*crossing to* R *of the sofa*) I'm glad you think so.

(HENRY *jerks* ROSITA *to her feet and pulls her across the front of Pamela to Flaherty*)

HENRY (*aside*) Come on. Get her out of here. Take her upstairs, Flaherty.

ROSITA. Dr Walling! I wish to be examined. Now.

FLAHERTY. Come on. Or I'll trample all over yer scorpions.

(FLAHERTY *takes* ROSITA *by the hand and pulls her off* R)

HENRY (*hissing after them*) Flaherty, watch out for the inspector. And find that damned cup.

PAMELA (*icily*) Henry! Could I have your attention for one minute.

HENRY (*absently*) Oh, sit down, Pamela. (*He hisses*) Put her back in the study and get Sarah to look after her. (*He gives one anxious look off* R, *closes the door then crosses to the sideboard and pours a drink for himself*)

(PAMELA *watches him, bewildered*)

(*He suddenly becomes conscious of Pamela*) Have a drink, Pam?

PAMELA. I don't drink in the mornings. I wasn't aware that you did, either.

HENRY. It's nearly afternoon. (*He crosses to the hall door and listens*)

PAMELA. I'm waiting for your explanation, Henry.

HENRY. Ah, yes. I'll show you to the door.

PAMELA. You'll what! Henry, when I came in, you were writhing on that settee with a girl.

HENRY. Oh, yes, she's a patient of mine—father fixation.

PAMELA. I see. Do you realize I've been waiting for you for the past three hours?

HENRY. I'm awfully sorry. I was going to telephone you, Pamela —several times.

PAMELA. Once would have been adequate.

HENRY. But things cropped up. (*Suddenly, as though he has a bright idea*) Pamela, why don't you go over to your uncle's and wait. Then as soon as Flaherty has taken his sack out, I'll collect you. Ssh! (*He opens the door* R *a little and peeps out*) Damn! They've gone upstairs. (*He closes the door*)

PAMELA (*moving up* C) Henry, could I have your attention for two consecutive minutes? Who is Flaherty?

HENRY (*moving to* R *of Pamela*) He was here just now—you met him.

PAMELA. Do you mean that dirty-looking man with the black face?

HENRY. That's the fellow. Quite a nice chap, really. Intelligent, too—reads the *New Statesman*.

PAMELA. Is he one of your patients?

HENRY. No—he's a sweep.

PAMELA. A sweep!

HENRY. Yes. They clean chimneys with brushes, you know, they screw them into each other like a fishing-rod and shove them up the chimney. You *must* know. (*He moves to the hall door*)

PAMELA. Will you stop drivelling and explain why the sweep and his bag should prevent us from going to the country for the week-end.

(HENRY *listens at the door*)

And come away from that damned door.

HENRY. Yes, dear. Of course, Pamela, I owe you an apology. (*He goes to Pamela and leads her to the sofa*) Please sit down.

PAMELA. You mean I can actually *stay* here? (*She sits on the sofa, at the left end of it*)

HENRY (*sitting on the right arm of the sofa*) For a minute or two. (*He pauses, then gives her his full attention*) Pamela, how much do you love me?

PAMELA. Do you think this is the time or place to go into that?

HENRY. No, but I must talk to you in a serious vein. Will you promise to be quiet and listen?

PAMELA. If you promise me that you don't intend to demonstrate how to sweep a chimney again.

HENRY. No. This concerns us. Pamela darling, I don't have to tell you what I think of you. To me you are . . .

(FLAHERTY *enters from the hall and stands by the open door*)

FLAHERTY. Psst.

HENRY (*rising and moving to Flaherty*) What is it?

FLAHERTY. They're on the first floor. Both your sisters and the inspector.

HENRY. When they go up to the top floor, let Rosita out and get the—(*he looks at Pamela*) get the other.

FLAHERTY. Sure. It's thirsty work, though. (*He crosses to the side-board and pours a drink*) I'll have a nip. This is your intended?

HENRY. Eh? Oh, yes. Pamela dear, this is Mr Flaherty—Miss Colefax.

FLAHERTY. How do you do?

HENRY. Pamela, you don't mind Mr Flaherty having a drink, do you?

FLAHERTY. Here's to the both of you. (*He drinks, then puts down the glass and crosses to the hall door*) I'll wait be the door here. (*He leans on the doorpost*) Go ahead with your talking. I doubt it'll be anythin' an old feller like meself shouldn't hear.

PAMELA (*with heavy geniality*) Dr Walling had just asked me how much I loved him. He was about to tell me what I meant to him.

FLAHERTY (*nodding approvingly*) Tell the girl, Dr Walling. Don't be keepin' her in suspense.

HENRY. Flaherty, go and wait in the hall.

PAMELA (*rising and moving* C) No, don't be so unsociable, Henry. Sit down, Mr Flaherty—Henry will show you how to sweep a chimney.

HENRY (*moving to* R *of Pamela*) You mustn't be upset, Pamela.

PAMELA (*moving* L) Upset? Why should I be upset? What could be pleasanter than to be kept waiting three hours; to be practically thrown out of the house as soon as I arrive and then further entertained by drinking Vat sixty-nine with the sweep?

HENRY. As soon as he's taken his sack out we can go.

FLAHERTY (*glancing into the hall*) Quiet! I think it's moving they are. I'll go and see. Excuse me for now.

PAMELA. Very well. Don't be too long.

(FLAHERTY *gives Pamela a look and exits to the hall.* HENRY *moves to the hall door*)

HENRY (*calling after Flaherty*) Be careful, man.

(PAMELA *moves to the sideboard and pours a drink for herself*)

(*He turns*) Pamela, where . . . ? Oh, there you are. I say, you're drinking in the morning.

PAMELA. The afternoon.

HENRY. Pamela dear, I'm awfully sorry.

PAMELA. No, don't say anything, Henry. Just sit down. I'll talk for a change.

HENRY. Yes, dear. (*He crosses to the easy chair down* L *and sits*)

PAMELA (*moving down* C) Leaving aside Mr Flaherty's sack, which seems altogether too complicated—and before you tell me again how much you love me, or what a pleasant man Mr Flaherty is, there is one small point that I should like clearing up. (*She puts her glass on the coffee-table*) Who is that little—Lolita you have now safely locked upstairs?

HENRY. It's Rosita Hernandez. She's a patient of mine.

PAMELA (*heavily*) So you said. And why did you find it necessary to lock her up?

HENRY. She's run away from home. That's why the inspector thinks she might be hiding here.

Pamela (*crossing to* R *of Henry*) Then why not let the inspector take her away? Why all this creeping up and down stairs and hissing at the sweep?

Henry (*rising and crossing to* RC) I—I can't explain that. Pam, please go and wait for me at your uncle's.

Pamela. Oh, no. I'll wait here. I'm intrigued to know how much my future is going to be affected by that sweep's sack.

Henry. So am I. I mean, I can't say at the moment. (*He suddenly sees the shoe and picks it up*)

Pamela. What an offensive piece of footwear. Is it yours?

Henry. No. It's Joe Corona's.

Pamela. A friend of yours?

Henry. Not exactly. He's a very old friend of my father's. We like to have something to remember him by. (*He puts the shoe on the table behind the sofa*)

Pamela. You certainly wouldn't forget him with that about the place. Henry, I'm trying to be patient. (*She crosses to him*) Tomorrow afternoon I'm supposed to be jumping in Sussex. Will you be taking me or not?

Henry. Well, Pam . . .

(Flaherty *enters from the hall*)

Flaherty (*moving to* R *of Henry*) He's searchin' a cupboard on the landing there.

Henry. Why the devil didn't Cynthia take him right up? What is he saying?

(Flaherty *goes to the hall door and listens*)

Flaherty. I can't quite catch it. I'm a little on the deaf side—soot in me ears, you know.

Henry. You're not deaf if anybody mentions anything over a five-pound note. (*He crosses to the hall door*) I'll see what I can hear.

Pamela. Henry, before you go . . .

Henry. Back in a minute.

(Henry *glares at Flaherty and exits to the hall*)

Flaherty (*crossing to the sideboard*) Will you have another?

Pamela. No, thank you. (*She sits on the sofa*)

Flaherty (*pouring a drink*) Little and often, that's me. You'd be Miss Colefax, the show jumper.

Pamela (*with considerable surprise*) I am.

Flaherty (*crossing to the easy chair* RC *and sitting*) Thought I'd seen you. I've a nephew in the Irish Army you might know—Captain Dermot Shea.

Pamela (*with respect, and still surprised*) Dermot Shea is your *nephew?*

Flaherty. He is. I mind him when he was a lad. I'd be out with him on the Curragh to see the sun rise, and the dew glistening the grass. Every morning for months in the summer we'd be there. He was a great lad for horses.

PAMELA. But he's superb! I saw him win the European Championship.

FLAHERTY. I'd say he was lucky there. I thought the Italian had the beating of him.

PAMELA. Oh, no! He was in a class on his own. I've tried dozens of times to get him to appear at different gymkhanas, but he's always engaged.

FLAHERTY. He's in demand right enough now. Independent, too. Would you like me to ask him for you?

PAMELA (*rising; excitedly*) You—you couldn't! Do you really think you *could?*

FLAHERTY. I'll whale the living daylights out of him if he won't.

PAMELA (*crossing to* L *of Flaherty*) Mr Flaherty! I could kiss you—even with your soot.

FLAHERTY. Don't let a bit of soot stop you.

PAMELA. You're the most wonderful sweep that ever lived. (*She kisses him*) There.

(SYBIL *enters from the kitchen as Pamela is kissing Flaherty*)

SYBIL (*crossing to* C) I wouldn't do that, Pamela, you'll get black.

(PAMELA *moves up* RC. FLAHERTY *rises*)

(*To Flaherty*) Have you brought Joe down?

FLAHERTY. They're still at the cupboard on the landing. Mr Walling is listening on the stairs.

SYBIL. Oh, dear. That sergeant will be through in a minute. He seems to get on *very* well with Mrs D'Arcy. (*She crosses to the hall door*) I'm going to see what's what—I don't trust Henry, he isn't himself today.

(SYBIL *exits to the hall*)

PAMELA (*moving to the sofa and sitting*) I don't trust him myself. He's in a terrible state. Although he seems more *human*, somehow. Do you find him remote, Mr Flaherty?

FLAHERTY (*moving to* R *of the sofa*) That's strange. Sarah was implyin' the same thing about yourself. Is it aloof you are?

PAMELA. Not really. It's just that Henry and Cynthia are so *clever*. I feel I have to impress them all the time. And there's nothing I can do—except ride a horse.

FLAHERTY. And what better thing for a woman to do.

PAMELA. I always feel on the defensive here. I never can understand what they are talking about. For instance, why is it so important that your sack should be brought down? Who is Joe—the police inspector?

FLAHERTY (*rising*) No. It's not the inspector. Joe's in the sack.

PAMELA. What *do* you mean?

Flaherty. Miss Colefax—are you set on marrying Dr Walling?

Pamela. Determined.

Flaherty (*crossing above the sofa to the fireplace*) I'd like to tell you a little story. When me brother Patrick married, his wife Maggie never knew that he had a poachin' case hangin' over him in the next county. In fact, he spent his honeymoon alone in the county jail—they let him out for the service.

Pamela. Has Henry been poaching?

Flaherty. No. What I'm tryin' to tell you is that there should be no secrets between man and wife.

Pamela. And Henry has a guilty secret. The girl? Or the sack?

Flaherty. The sack.

Pamela. I see. What's in it?

Flaherty. I told you. Joe Corona. The feller that shoe belongs to—I found him up the chimney.

Pamela (*gulping*) Dead, I presume?

Flaherty. As Napoleon, ma'am.

Pamela. Then it isn't anyone Henry has murdered—unless he was a juvenile delinquent.

Flaherty (*sitting* L *of Pamela on the sofa*) It's a crook who tried to kill the father—some sort of an accident, I understand.

Pamela. Are the police looking for the body or the girl?

Flaherty. The girl. I hope to God she doesn't look in the sack—it's in the room with her.

Pamela. And you're co-operating in disposing of Mr Corona. It's awfully kind of you.

Flaherty. Ah, well, there's a bit in it for me. Maybe I shouldn't have told you. They may dock me money, but I think you should know. I'd say you're a sensible girl.

Pamela. Thank you. I'm glad in a way this has happened. I've never seen Henry with his hair down before.

(Henry *and* Sybil *enter from the hall.* Flaherty *rises*)

Sybil (*moving* RC) Mr Flaherty, they've gone up to the top floor. Come along. I'll look after Rosita. Henry, watch the sergeant. What *can* he be doing with Mrs D'Arcy?

(Flaherty *and* Sybil *exit to the hall.* Henry *crosses to the kitchen door, opens it, looks off, then goes to the sideboard and pours a drink*)

Henry. I'm sorry about this, Pamela, but I did ask you to go. (*He drinks*)

Pamela. I'm quite comfortable. You won't be able to drive if you have any more of that.

Henry (*crossing to* RC) You have no idea what I've been through. If only I could tell you.

Pamela. Why don't you?

Henry. No, it's impossible. (*Suddenly*) Pamela, I can't marry you.

PAMELA. Why not?

HENRY. It wouldn't do. (*He sits on the left arm of the easy chair* RC)

PAMELA. Shouldn't I be the judge of that?

HENRY. No. You don't have the evidence. There are—well, things in our family history that would shock you.

PAMELA. What about my family history? Sir Rupert Colefax walled up four Roundheads—alive.

HENRY. He what?

PAMELA. He built a chimney round them. We never knew which one.

HENRY. He *did?* (*He rises and moves to* R *of the sofa*) That's wonderful! Did you say a chimney?

PAMELA. You won't hold it against me, Henry?

HENRY. No. (*Slowly*) But it all happened years ago. It was nothing to do with you.

PAMELA. Any more than you had anything to do with Joe Corona.

HENRY. No, I'll give you that, but . . . (*He does a sudden "take"*) What do you know about him?

PAMELA. Nothing. Except that he was up your chimney and now he's in Flaherty's bag.

HENRY. Pamela! Who told you? Flaherty! It must have been. I'll murder the garrulous swine. He swore he wouldn't say a word. *Encyclopaedia!* I wouldn't buy him an evening paper. (*He crosses to the fireplace*)

PAMELA. I'm glad he told me. I feel I owe a debt to Joe Corona, too.

HENRY. What are you saying, Pamela? You're not well. How can you say such a thing?

PAMELA. It's true. Joe Corona has changed you from a cold, clinical and rather prim psychiatrist into a human being.

HENRY. You're mad!

PAMELA (*rising and moving to him*) Don't start analysing me. What if I were a little mad—you need someone like that to keep you in shape.

HENRY. I've never heard you talk like this . . .

PAMELA. I've been too scared of you, before. (*She kisses him*) Now—(*briskly*) let's help Flaherty get Joe out of here and drive off and have a jolly week-end.

HENRY. I—I don't know what to say.

PAMELA. Then don't say anything. For once you don't have the correct phrase on the tip of your tongue.

(*There is a knock at the front door*)

HENRY. Who is that?

PAMELA. Why not open the door and find out?

HENRY (*crossing to* C) Good idea, old girl. (*He stops*) No. I must stay and keep that sergeant from upstairs.

(Paul *storms in from the hall.*

Sybil *follows him on.* Pamela *sits on the sofa.* Henry *moves up* c)

Paul (*crossing to* c) I want to see Sarah.

Sybil. No, no, Paul. I'm sorry but she's busy.

Paul. That's too bad.

Sybil. You can't see Sarah now, Paul. Come back this afternoon.

Paul. I've been getting the brush-off all week-end. I'll wait until she's ready.

Henry. Paul!

Paul. Don't you start! What's wrong with me—am I a leper or something?

Sybil. No, Paul, we like you.

Henry (*crossing to the fireplace*) Speak for yourself.

Paul. Now, listen, you—just because you're engaged to some horse-faced female with a pedigree, Sarah mustn't be seen with anyone who doesn't make *Debrett.*

Henry. Watch it, Mr Martell!

Pamela. Is this Sarah's young man?

Paul. Yes. Who are you? Miss Debrett in person?

Pamela. Yes. Don't bother to kneel.

Paul. I won't. I intend to sit down and wait for Sarah. (*He sits on the right arm of the sofa and lights a cigarette*)

(*There is a moment's awkward pause*)

Henry (*crossing above the sofa to* c; *more graciously*) Now look, Paul old man, there's nothing personal in this. We're having a private family discussion. One of my patients has escaped.

Paul. The best of luck to them. Is that why the police car is outside?

Henry. Yes, that's right. (*He moves to* r *of Paul and takes his arm*) So if you wouldn't mind . . .

Paul (*rising*) I don't mind. I can cope with lunatics. I'm getting plenty of practice.

Pamela. Let him stay, Henry.

Paul (*moving above the sofa*) Thank you, your ladyship—I intend to. (*He picks up the shoe*) Your friend called for his shoe, yet, Mrs Walling?

(Henry *moves to* r *of Paul and takes the shoe from him*)

Sybil. I beg your pardon?

Henry (*replacing the shoe on the table*) No, no, he hasn't, but he may be here any minute. That's another reason why we'd like you to go.

Paul (*crossing to the fireplace*) Didn't see anyone hopping down the road as I came along.

(HARDY *and* CYNTHIA *enter from the hall.* SYBIL *crosses and sits* R *of Pamela on the sofa*)

HARDY (*as he enters*) Sorry to have bothered you, miss. She's obviously not here.

CYNTHIA. I never thought she was.

HARDY. Well, we'll get along, then. (*He crosses to* R *of Sybil*) Mrs Walling, if you do find that body you'll let us know, won't you? Is the sergeant still outside?

SYBIL. He was talking with Mrs D'Arcy.

HARDY (*moving up* LC) I'll get him. Well, Dr Walling, thank you for all your co-operation. (*He moves to the kitchen door*) Might as well go out this way. Good day.

ALL (*ad lib*) Good-bye.

(HARDY *exits to the kitchen*)

SYBIL. What a relief! Cynthia, rush up and tell Flaherty the police have gone.

(SARAH *enters from the hall.*
CYNTHIA *exits to the hall, bumping into Sarah as she goes*)

They've *gone*, Sarah.

SARAH. Thank goodness. (*She sees Paul*) Paul! (*She moves* C) What are you doing here?

PAUL (*crossing to Sarah*) I'm waiting for you. Ready?

SARAH. Well, er—not just now, Paul.

PAUL. You're coming now. (*He leads Sarah tc the garden door*) I'm sick of your family keeping you away from me.

SARAH. Now, Paul . . .

(HARDY *enters from the kitchen*)

HARDY (*as he enters*) Dr Walling, I wonder . . .

PAUL (*to Sarah*) Don't argue. You're coming. Yesterday you couldn't come because your father's old study was being decorated. Today it's escaped lunatics and the sweep again. I've had enough. If you don't have a mind of your own, I'll think for you.

HARDY. Just a minute, sir. (*To Henry*) Dr Walling, did I understand this young man to say that your father's study was being decorated yesterday?

HENRY. Yes.

HARDY. The door was open then?

HENRY. Y-yes.

HARDY. I understood you to say it hadn't been opened for twenty years.

HENRY. Oh, Rosita couldn't be there. The decorators never left it empty.

HARDY. Didn't they go out for lunch?

HENRY. Y-e-e-e . . .

HARDY. The girl was missing yesterday, wasn't she? I think I'll take a look. (*He crosses to the hall door*)

HENRY. You can't.

HARDY. Why not?

HENRY. We've lost the key.

HARDY. Then the door will have to be forced. If she has been there since yesterday, heaven knows *what* condition she is in by now.

HENRY (*crossing to* C) Now, look here, Inspector, this is ridiculous.

HARDY. Come, come, Dr Walling . . .

SYBIL. But, Inspector, the lock on that door is an heirloom.

HARDY (*producing a bunch of keys*) Perhaps these will do the trick. You better come, Dr Walling.

(HARDY *exits to the hall.*
HENRY *looks wildly around, then dashes off after Hardy*)

PAMELA (*rising*) Henry! Wait for me!

(PAMELA *dashes off* R)

PAUL. What *is* going on here?

SARAH. Paul! You *must* go.

(*There is a yell from* MRS D'ARCY *off in the kitchen*)

SYBIL (*rising and moving to the kitchen door*) Good heavens! What was that?

SARAH (*moving to Sybil*) We'd better go and see. Paul, please go.

SYBIL. I hate to think what they might have found.

(SYBIL *and* SARAH *exit to the kitchen, leaving Paul on his own*)

PAUL. Sarah!

(FLAHERTY *enters from the hall, pushing* ROSITA *before him. She still carries her parcel*)

FLAHERTY (*leading Rosita up* C) Now, stay there, and when the inspector comes down—you've only just arrived, you understand now?

ROSITA. Yes, I understand. But when can I see Dr Walling alone?

FLAHERTY. When the inspector comes down with him. (*To Paul*) Hello, there. Watch her for me, will you? I have to collect my sack —the Lord protect us.

(FLAHERTY *exits to the hall*)

PAUL (*moving to* L *of Rosita*) So you're the character who's causing all this fuss.

(ROSITA *backs* R)

I can see their point.

ROSITA. Please, sir, do not arrest me and take me back to my father. He will send me back to Aragua.

PAUL. Where?

ROSITA. I have to stay in England to be cured by Dr Walling. He understands me. (*Winningly*) Do you *have* to arrest me?

PAUL. No, not really.

ROSITA. Oh, thank you, thank you. (*She throws herself into his arms*)

PAUL (*after a pause*) Don't mention it. Have you had lunch?

ROSITA. No. I'm very hungry.

PAUL. So am I. Look, why not come with me and tell me all about it over lunch. I'm determined to eat with *someone*.

ROSITA. Your inspector won't mind.

PAUL. No, not in the least. Come along. (*He pushes Rosita out by the garden door*) This way.

(ROSITA *exits by the garden door.*
BRAY *enters from the kitchen. He looks very shamefaced and is rubbing his cheek*)

(*To Bray*) Good afternoon.

BRAY. Good afternoon, sir.

(PAUL *exits by the garden door.*
SYBIL, MRS D'ARCY *and* SARAH *enter from the kitchen.* MRS D'ARCY *is holding her nose and is very angry*)

MRS D'ARCY. He ought to be arrested.

BRAY (*moving up* RC) I've said I'm sorry.

SYBIL (*crossing to* C) Pulling the poor woman's nose. What made you do it?

BRAY. I *had* to. It was my duty.

MRS D'ARCY. Your duty! Buttering me up with all that talk, then suddenly he makes a grab at me nose. I'd be better treated if I was in the zoo.

SARAH. You don't just suddenly, out of the blue, pull someone's nose, Sergeant. Why?

BRAY (*impatiently*) I thought it would come off.

MRS D'ARCY. Come off! Well, of all the nerve. (*She moves and looks in the mirror*) I only hope you haven't damaged the filaments.

SARAH. Where's Paul?

BRAY. The young man? (*He indicates the garden door*) He went out that way as I came in.

SARAH. Oh, *dear!* I'll see if I can calm him down.

(SARAH *rushes out by the garden door*)

BRAY (*to Mrs D'Arcy*) I'm sorry, madam. But suppose you were a criminal—in hiding?

MRS D'ARCY. Listen to him! I'm a criminal, now.

(HARDY *enters from the hall.*
CYNTHIA, HENRY *and* PAMELA *follow him on. They are exchanging bewildered glances.* HENRY *stands* RC. PAMELA *and* CYNTHIA *stand* R)

HARDY (*crosses to* C) Never take anything for granted, Dr Walling. You see, the door was wide open. And everyone was certain it was locked.

HENRY. Y-yes.

HARDY. We'll go now, Sergeant. What's the matter with you?

BRAY. I might as well tell you before anyone else does. I pulled her nose.

HARDY. Whose nose?

MRS D'ARCY. Whose do you think? (*She crosses to Hardy*) To see if it would come off, if you ever heard such a thing. I'm going to report him.

(BRAY *moves up* R)

HARDY (*sternly*) Sergeant, you must learn to control yourself. (*To Mrs D'Arcy*) On the other hand, ma'am, in a way, he was only doing his job.

MRS D'ARCY. Pulling my nose? He wouldn't like to kick my teeth in, I suppose?

HARDY. Mrs D'Arcy, we have a long list of criminals who frequently change their apperance. Dyed hair, false noses, you'd be surprised what they get up to. The sergeant, of course, overreached himself.

MRS D'ARCY. I'll say he did! Right over the cooker.

(MRS D'ARCY *exits to the kitchen.* SYBIL *moves to* L *of the sofa*)

HENRY (*crossing to the sideboard*) Ah, well—if you really have finished, Inspector, will you both have a drink before you go? (*He pours two drinks*)

HARDY. I'll have a small whisky, if it's all the same to you. The sergeant doesn't drink. No use waiting till you're off duty. You never are on our job.

HENRY (*handing a drink to Hardy*) I suppose not.

HARDY. Why, a few moments ago your mother mentioned the name—Joe Corona.

(HENRY *reacts, spilling his drink*)

At first I couldn't think when I'd come across it before. Then I remembered. It's been on our "Wanted List" of Missing Persons for twenty years or more. But as I always say to the sergeant here, "Keep your eyes open, you never know, he may be under our very noses at this moment."

(FLAHERTY *enters from the hall, carrying a filled sack*)

FLAHERTY. Oh! Good Lord above . . . ! (*He crosses towards the garden door*)

(*The others stand petrified*)

HARDY. No, don't go.

(FLAHERTY *stops* R *of Hardy*)

(*He smiles at Henry*) There might be a body in there.

SYBIL. There is.

HARDY. I thought so. I wonder what made you think of that name "Corona", Mrs Walling? Was it reading about his old gang leader, Sam Vespata?

SYBIL. I—I—don't quite know.

HARDY. As a matter of fact, we deported Sam back to Malta several years ago. He died there last week.

(SYBIL *stares out front*)

Must have been that which brought the name to mind. (*He looks at Sybil*) Don't you worry, Mrs Walling, if it isn't Joe Corona in that sack it might be some other crook. (*He winks at Bray*) You never know your luck, do you? Come along, Sergeant, we'd better take the body with us.

(BRAY *takes the sack from Flaherty*)

No need to drag it through the hall. (*He indicates the garden door*) This way. Oh, and Dr Walling, if you do hear from Miss Hernandez, you'll give us a call at Scotland Yard, won't you? You know our number, I take it?

(HARDY *and* BRAY *exit by the garden door*)

HENRY (*dazed*) He's—he's c-carried it out himself. (*He pours another large drink for himself*)

FLAHERTY (*crossing to Henry*) Save some of that for me, will yer, sir. I'd like to be lubricated before they take me.

PAMELA (*moving up* C) Henry, you must go out there and stop them, or you, Flaherty.

FLAHERTY. No, not me, miss. I'm thinking of getting the midnight mail to Dublin.

SYBIL (*emerging from her trance*) Sam Vespata is dead!

HENRY. To hell with Sam Vespata! You've put us all in the clink for the rest of our lives.

(SARAH *enters from the garden*)

SARAH (*moving down* RC) The two policemen are just driving off.

HENRY. They'll be back.

SARAH. Oh, no, they won't. They've just dumped the sack on Flaherty's cart.

FLAHERTY (*moving* C) You mean—they—they've left it on me cart, without even lookin' in it?

SARAH. Yes. Good old Joe! (*She sits in the easy chair* RC)

(PAMELA *moves to* HENRY *who puts his arms around her.* CYNTHIA *crosses and sits in the easy chair* L)

FLAHERTY. Well, I'd better be off. I know just the spot for to put him. I'll be round about the *Encyclopaedia* and me house, of course. (*He picks up the shoe*) Might as well let Joe take his shoe with him—I'll pop it in the sack. One of the most exciting chimneys it's been my pleasure to sweep.

(FLAHERTY *waves cheerily and exits to the garden*)

SYBIL (*rising*) Sam Vespata. Sam Vespata. (*She crosses to the telephone*) I must ring Scotland. (*She lifts the receiver*)

HENRY. Now, it's all right, Mother dear. No need to worry any more.

SYBIL (*into the telephone*) Operator, I want a personal call, please, to B. McDonald, Inverness three-o-nine-seven-six . . . Yes . . . This is Heath three-o-four-nine . . . Yes, I'll hold on . . .

HENRY. Mother, surely you aren't ringing Mrs McDonald now?

SYBIL. Mrs McDonald, dear? Who's she? (*She laughs*)

HENRY (*to the others*) The shock's been too much for her. You know Mrs McDonald. You spend six months of the year with her.

SYBIL. No, dear. I spend six months of the year with your father. (*Into the telephone*) Hello, dear . . . Great news . . . Sam Vespata is dead . . . He died in Malta last week . . . Really . . . You can come home tonight . . .

CURTAIN

FURNITURE AND PROPERTY LIST

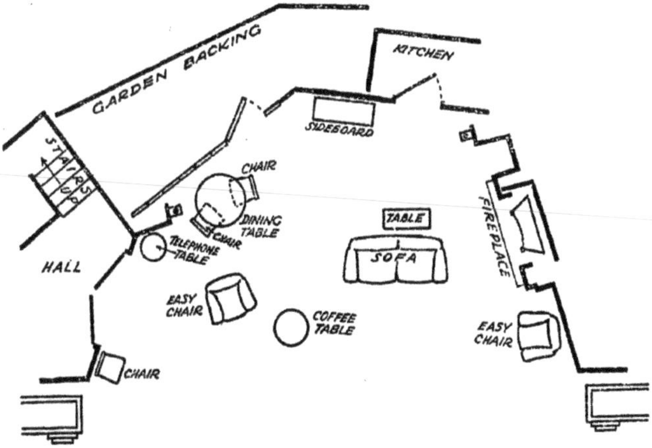

ACT I

On stage: Upright chair (down R)
Small table (R) *On it:* telephone, ashtray
2 upright chairs (up RC)
Dining-table. *On it:* white cloth, transistor radio, vase of flowers, ashtray, copy of *The Stage*, napkin ring, 2 cups, 2 saucers, 2 teaspoons, 2 small plates, 2 knives, tray with pot of coffee, jug of milk, sugar, pot of marmalade, butter, rack with toast
On floor beside table: napkin
Easy chair (RC) *On it:* cushion
Coffee-table (down C)
Sofa. *On it:* cushions
Table (behind sofa) *On it:* ashtray, lighter
Sideboard. *On it:* table-lamp, ashtray, vase of flowers, box of cigars, tray with bottle of Vat 69 whisky, bottle of gin, bottle of wine, 6 glasses
In cupboard: bottles, bottle of Vat 69
Easy chair (down L) *On it:* cushion
Firegrate
Over mantelpiece: mirror
On mantelpiece: clock, ornaments, ashtray, invitation cards, Cynthia's spectacles, packet of cigarettes, lighter
Carpet on floor

Off stage: Drawer. *In it:* old papers, photographs, etc. (CYNTHIA)
Copy of the *New Statesman* (FLAHERTY)
Letter (MRS D'ARCY)
Brief-case (HENRY)
Sweep's brushes (FLAHERTY)
Sacks (FLAHERTY)
Shoe (FLAHERTY)
Flashlight (FLAHERTY)
Cup of coffee (SARAH)

Personal: FLAHERTY: spectacles
HENRY: wallet

ACT II

Strike: Dirty glasses
Coffee cup
Drawer with papers, etc.
Brief-case
Shoe

Reset: Drinks tray on sideboard with clean glasses

Set: *On sofa:* magazine, transistor radio
On table: bowl of fruit
On mantelpiece: key
Tidy room generally

Off stage: Carton (PAUL)
Towels (MRS D'ARCY)
Delivery note (PAUL)
3 cartons (PAUL)
Book wrapped in paper (FLAHERTY)
Tray with coffee for four (MRS D'ARCY)
Brushes (FLAHERTY)
Shoe (MRS D'ARCY)
Parcel. *In it:* silver cup (ROSITA)
Filled sack (FLAHERTY)

ACT III

Setting as at the end of the previous Act

Off stage: Tray of tea for one (Cynthia)

Personal: Paul: cigarettes, lighter
Hardy: bunch of keys
Filled sack (Flaherty)

LIGHTING PLOT

Property fittings required: table-lamp (non-practical) firegrate

Interior. A morning-room. The same scene throughout

The Apparent Source of Light is a large window back c

The Main Acting Areas are up c, down r, down l, c, at an easy chair rc and at a sofa lc

ACT I. Morning

To open: Effect of summer sunshine

No cues

ACT II. Morning

To open: Effect of summer sunshine

No cues

ACT III. Morning

To open: Lights as at the end of the previous Act

No cues

EFFECTS PLOT

ACT I

Cue 1	At rise of CURTAIN *Music of "Pop" number from transistor radio*	(Page 1)
Cue 2	SARAH switches off transistor *Stop music*	(Page 1)
Cue 3	CYNTHIA: ". . . that breakfast table." *Front door opens and closes*	(Page 4)
Cue 4	CYNTHIA: ". . . until he's finished." *Thud from above*	(Page 9)
Cue 5	HENRY: ". . . father's old study." *Thud from above*	(Page 9)
Cue 6	HENRY: "I must *think*." *Telephone rings*	(Page 14)

ACT II

Cue 7	At rise of CURTAIN *Music from transistor radio*	(Page 24)
Cue 8	After rise of CURTAIN *Knock on front door*	(Page 24)
Cue 9	SARAH switches off transistor *Stop music*	(Page 24)
Cue 10	SARAH: "Oh!" *Two thuds off* R	(Page 24)
Cue 11	PAUL: "Oh!" *Front door slams*	(Page 27)
Cue 12	HENRY: ". . . he wasn't hurt." *Telephone rings*	(Page 36)
Cue 13	FLAHERTY: ". . . see Dr Walling." *Knock at front door*	(Page 45)

Cue 14 MRS D'ARCY looks in mirror (Page 45)
Knock at front door

ACT III

Cue 15 FLAHERTY: ". . . at Scotland Yard." (Page 56)
Knock at front door

Cue 16 PAMELA: ". . . of your tongue." (Page 63)
Knock at front door

Milton Keynes UK
Ingram Content Group UK Ltd.
UKHW020645100124
435784UK00013B/281

9 780573 010583